Gozo

inu Church

ozo Citadel
Cathedral ● St George's Church ● Ggantija

Mistra Rocks
(Gebel Mistra)

**GOZO &
CAMINO**

Cominotto
(Kemmunett)

Comino
(Kemmuna) ●

D1485867

nella

'alace
Museum

abbar

Marsaskala ●

VALLETTA
Auberge de Castile et Léon
Bibliotheca
Casa Rocca Piccola
Church of St Paul's Shipwreck
Fort St Elmo
Grandmaster's Palace
Lascaris War Rooms
Manoel Theatre
Misrah Ir-Repubblika
National Museum of Archaeology
National Museum of Fine Arts
National War Museum
Sacra Infemeria
St John's Co-Cathedral & Museum
Upper Barrakka Gardens
La Vittoria

TWINPACK
Malta & Gozo

LINDSAY BENNETT

AA Publishing
If you have any comments or suggestions for this guide you can contact the editor at
travelguides@TheAA.com

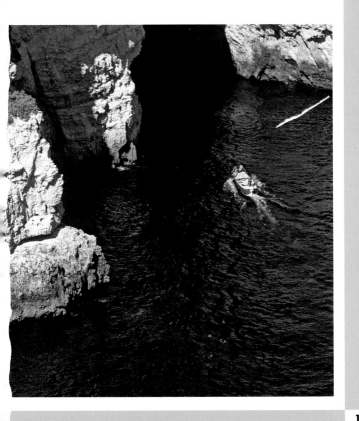

How to Use This Book

KEY TO SYMBOLS

➕ Map reference

✉ Address

☎ Telephone number

🕐 Opening/closing times

🍴 Restaurant or café

🚉 Nearest rail station

🚌 Nearest bus route

⛴ Nearest riverboat or ferry stop

♿ Facilities for visitors with disabilities

❓ Other practical information

▷ Further information

ℹ Tourist information

✋ Admission charges: Expensive (over €8), Moderate (€5–€8), and Inexpensive (under €5)

★ Major Sight   ★ Minor Sight

👣 Walks   🚍 Drives

🏬 Shops

🎭 Entertainment and Activities

🍴 Restaurants

This guide is divided into four sections

• Essential Malta & Gozo: An introduction to the islands and tips on making the most of your stay.

• Malta & Gozo by Area: We've broken the island into four areas, and recommended the best sights, shops, activities, restaurants, entertainment and nightlife venues in each one. Suggested walks and drives help you to explore.

• Where to Stay: The best hotels, whether you're looking for luxury, budget or something in between.

• Need to Know: The info you need to make your trip run smoothly, including getting about by public transport, weather tips, emergency phone numbers and useful websites.

Navigation In the Malta & Gozo by Area chapter, we've given each area its own colour, which is also used on the locator maps throughout the book and the map on the inside front cover.

Maps The fold-out map accompanying this book is a comprehensive map of Malta & Gozo. The grid on this fold-out map is the same as the grid on the locator maps within the book. The grid references to these maps are shown with capital letters (A1); those to the town plan are shown with lower-case letters (a1).

Contents

Introducing Malta & Gozo

Long languid summers and bright fresh winters provide a backdrop to Malta's wealth of natural and cultural attractions—many that are unique and unmissable. Yet you can just as easily sit by the pool, head to the spa or go clubbing.

This tiny island nation sits almost at the centre of the Mediterranean Sea and this location has been instrumental in the Malta story. Physically shaped by the power of the surrounding water, an impressive slab of limestone with monumental cliffs and myriad caves, its history has been moulded by the tides of humanity that have wound up on these shores. It has been at the centre of conflict and cooperation since civilization came to the Mediterranean basin, and it has played a vital role at pivotal moments in history; the landscape scattered with tantalizing reminders of this past, dating from the very start of man's ability to build in stone.

Despite being influenced by Phoenicians, Carthaginians, Romans, Byzantines, Arabs, Sicilians, the Aragonese, and latterly the Knights of St. John and the British, the Maltese culture remains distinctive. Christianity took a hold early, and it is still the backbone of modern society.

Today tourism earns the daily bread. Visitors are drawn by the eons of history, magnificent architecture and prized art, but the Maltese know these aren't the only ingredients that make a magical trip. Add luxury hotels, great restaurants, professional service and a genial attitude and you complete the picture. Malta is a great place to get active, with coastal footpaths and bridleways, and it's a centre of excellence for scuba diving.

Don't be surprised if you run into a film crew somewhere around the island during your visit. Productions bring in millions of dollars of foreign earnings. Home to the world-renowned Mediterranean Film Studios, Malta is the European 'Hollywood' and the island towns and villages are often a backdrop to period bodice-rippers and contemporary crime capers.

Facts + Figures

● The country of Malta consists of three islands: Malta at 246sq km (95sq miles); Gozo at 67sq km (25sq miles); Comino at only 3sq km (1sq mile).
● Malta lies 90km (56 miles) south of Sicily and 300km (180 miles) north of Libya.

LANGUAGE

Maltese is a Semitic language related to Arabic and Hebrew that developed in Malta, Sicily and the heel of Italy in medieval times. It's the only Semitic language written in the Latin alphabet and borrows half of its words from Latin/Italian. English is a co-national language.

THE KNIGHTS HOSPITALLERS

Without the influence of the Knights Hospitallers (Knights of St. John), Malta would probably look very different. Their wealth endowed civil and religious architecture, not just in their capital, Valletta, but all across the land during their tenure, between 1530 and 1798.

SIZE ISN'T EVERYTHING

Malta is the smallest country in the European Union but has the highest population density, at 1,308 people per square kilometre. It is the seventh densest state in the world, and the second most densely populated island in the world.

FESTAS

All towns and villages have at least one *festa* sometime between May and September, celebrating the local patron saint. These genuine Maltese experiences shouldn't be missed. The tourist office has a full list of *festas* (▷ 120).

A Short Stay in Malta & Gozo

DAY 1: VALLETTA

Morning Valletta is a city packed full of attractions, all of which must be reached on foot. Although it's compact, there are lots of inclines and flights of steps, so wear comfortable shoes. From the bus station, enter Valletta through the main gate at the top of the city. Visit the **National Museum of Archaeology** (▷ 32) and the **Church of St. Paul's Shipwreck** (▷ 25).

Mid-morning Stop for coffee and cake at **Caffe Cordina** (▷ 44), and then enter **St. John's Co-Cathedral** (▷ 35) for the dramatic Preti and Caravaggio paintings and funerary paraphernalia of the Knights.

Make your way to **Upper Barrakka Gardens** (▷ 39) in time to watch the firing of the noonday gun at the Gun Saluting Battery and to take in the views across **Grand Harbour** (▷ 28).

Lunch If you want to eat alfresco, you'll get great views and food from the roof terrace of **The Carriage** (▷ 44), but in inclement weather try **The Chef** (▷ 44) for it's excellent 'slow food'.

Afternoon Visit the state rooms in the **Grandmaster's Palace** (▷ 30) then walk down Republic Street to **Casa Rocca Piccola** (▷ 24), with its wealth of family knick-knacks. Stroll on to **Sacra Infermeria** (▷ 34). Across the street from here is the entrance to **The Malta Experience** (▷ 43) audiovisual spectacular.

Evening Take bus route 62 to **Sliema** (▷ 78). Stroll along the seafront and stop at one of the lively bars for a pre-dinner drink. For dinner, Maltese restaurant **Ta'Kris** (▷ 90) is a great introduction to local cuisine and has a lively atmosphere.

DAY 2: HYPOGEUM, TARXIEN TEMPLES, MDINA

Morning Immerse yourself in Malta's fascinating ancient history and see the best of the Temple Building Civilization. Reserve a place (pre-booking essential) at one of the early tours of the **Hypogeum** (▷ 50) underground temple and catacomb complex (bus routes 8, 11, 12, 27, 29, 30, 115), then walk on to the **Tarxien Temples** (▷ 54) before returning by bus to Valletta (routes 8, 11, 27, 29, 30). Move on by bus (routes 80 and 81) to the medieval hilltop town of **Mdina** (▷ 72) and have lunch here.

Lunch Fontanella Tea Garden (▷ 90) has a light menu with panoramic views, or try **Trattoria AD1530** (▷ 90), set in a medieval square.

Afternoon Stroll around the Silent City, enjoying the architecture and the art galleries, or take a horse-drawn carriage ride through the narrow streets. Make sure you visit the beautiful, baroque **St. Paul's Cathedral** (▷ 74) and the Norman **Palazzo Falson** (▷ 81), and spend some time relaxing and enjoying the spectacular views from Bastion Square. The **Medieval Times** (▷ 89) walk-through attraction gives a good indication of how life would have been during the era when Mdina was capital of Malta. **Domus Romana** (▷ 83), the remains of a Roman town house just outside the city gate, is worth a visit to view the mosaic floors if you have the time after your tour of Mdina.

Dinner The courtyard at **The Medina** (▷ 90) is a lovely location, or book a silver-service extravaganza at **Le Mondion** (▷ 90) at the Xara Palace Hotel, followed by a digestif at Fontanella Tea Garden.

Evening The streets of Mdina have a magical atmosphere in the evenings. Stay on for an early dinner, or return later.

Top 25

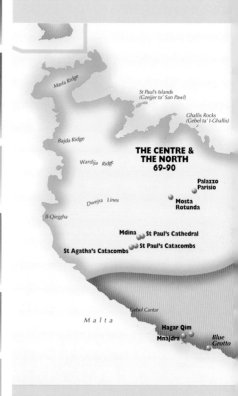

▶ ▶ ▶

**Azure Window and
Fungus Rock** ▷ 94
Vertiginous natural arch sur-
rounded by dazzling seas.

Blue Grotto ▷ 48
Dramatic rock formations,
caves and crystal clear,
azure waters.

Casa Rocca Piccola
▷ 24 A medieval palace
and family home filled with
antique furniture and art.

The Three Cities ▷ 56
The cities were the first
home of the Knights on
Malta with a naval heritage.

Tarxien Temples ▷ 54
Malta's largest prehistoric
temple complex, dating
from c.3600BC, displays the
architectural and decorative
art of the Temple Builders.

Sliema ▷ 78 The liveliest
and longest-established of
Malta's coastal resorts, with
luxury hotels and clubs.

**St. Johns Co-Cathedral
and Museum** ▷ 35
A majestic baroque interior,
home to Caravaggio's
signed masterpiece.

Sacra Infermeria ▷ 34
The medieval world's fin-
est hospital, built by the
Knights of St. John.

**Rabat: St. Paul's and
St. Agatha's Catacombs**
▷ 77 Underground Roman
and early Christian sites with
Byzantine frescoes.

Naxxar: Palazzo Parisio
▲ ▷ 76 Magnificent patrician
▲ palace and formal gardens
▲ in baroque style.

**National Museum of
Fine Arts** ▷ 33 Mattia
Preti leads the island's
premier collection.

**National Museum of
Archaeology** ▷ 32
A unique collection from
Malta's illustrious history.

Marfa Ridge

St Paul's Islands
(Gzejjer ta' San Pawl)

Ghallis Rocks
(Gebel ta' l-Ghallis)

Bajda Ridge

**THE CENTRE &
THE NORTH
69-90**

Wardija Ridge

Dwejra Lines

Il-Qlejgha

Palazzo
Parisio

Mosta
Rotunda

Mdina ● St Paul's Cathedral
● St Paul's Catacombs
St Agatha's Catacombs ●

Gebel Cantar

M a l t a

Hagar Qim ●

Mnajdra ● ● Blue
Grotto

ESSENTIAL MALTA & GOZO TOP 25

8

These pages are a quick guide to the Top 25, which are described in more detail later. Here they are listed alphabetically, and the tinted background shows which area they are in.

Church of St. Paul's Shipwreck ▷ 25 Much revered relics and a gilded wooden statue of the saint.

Comino ▷ 96 The tiny island getaway with the Blue Lagoon and wild countryside to explore.

Forts and Fortifications ▷ 26 An exceptional 16th-century citadel and Knights' headquarters.

Ġgantija ▷ 98 The oldest freestanding man-made structure in the world, comprising two temples.

Gozo Citadel ▷ 100 A fortified enclave oozing medieval atmosphere.

Grand Harbour ▷ 28 One of the world's finest natural inlets and a historic naval port.

Grandmaster's Palace ▷ 30 Headquarters of the Knights of St. John from the 1500s.

Ħaġar Qim & Mnajdra ▷ 49 Ancient hilltop temples to honour goddesses.

Hypogeum ▷ 50 Unique underground temple and catacomb complex, dating from 3600BC.

Marsaskala ▷ 52 Tourist town with charm set on a sheltered harbour in a narrow bay surrounded by dramatic headlands.

GOZO & CAMINO 91-106

Gozo

Azure Window
Gozo Citadel
Fungus Rock
Ghajn Abdul
Ġgantija
Mistra Rocks (Gebel Mistra)
Comino (Kemmuna)
Cominotto (Kemmunett)

VALLETTA 20-44

Sliema
Valletta
Grand Harbour
Vittoriosa
Senglea
Cospicua
Hypogeum
Tarxien Temples
Marsaskala

VALLETTA
Casa Rocca Piccola
Church of St Paul's Shipwreck
Forts & Fortifications
Grandmaster's Palace
National Museum of Archaeology
National Museum of Fine Arts
Sacra Infermeria
St John's Co-Cathedral & Museum

THE SOUTH 45-68

Mosta Rotunda ▷ 75 A 19th-century parish church with one of the largest domes in Europe.

Mdina: St Paul's Cathedral ▷ 74 A baroque tour de force created by Maltese masters.

Mdina ▷ 72 Medieval hilltop citadel in the heart of the island, with some spectacular views.

◄ ◄ ◄

Out and About

Malta's Mediterranean climate means lots of dry and sunny weather for outdoor activities. Certainly care needs to be taken during the heat of summer—the best season for taking to the water—but the other three seasons are ideal for a range of land-based sports and pastimes. Sports companies are well regulated by the Maltese authorities, so equipment and training is usually of a good standard.

Diving and Snorkelling

Malta is one of the best locations in the Mediterranean for scuba diving for several reasons. First, there's very little sand and sediment to make the water cloudy. Second, the limestone substrate has been eroded by the waves to give interesting and dramatic features. Third, there are many artificial dive sites, such as shipwrecks, to explore. Finally, the dive operations are professionally run. Sliema/St. Julian's, St. Paul's Bay, Marsalforn and Xlendi are the major locations of dive companies but the dive sites are scattered around the Maltese islands.

Boating and Sailing

Maltese coastal waters are magnificent and usually very calm in summer, so it's a lovely place for a morning or day boat trip. The main destination is the Blue Lagoon at Comino (▷ 97), which does get pretty crowded in peak season, but it's not to be missed. Alternatively, take a commercial trip or charter a boat with crew for the day. The marinas at

There are many different ways to explore the islands' natural resources, both energetic and leisurely

---

SOMETHING MORE EXTREME

Coasteering is the act of navigating around the intertidal zone without the aid of boats or kayaks. It may include walking on beaches, or more vigorous activities like climbing over rocks, jumping from low bluffs into the water or swimming through pools, depending on the actual topography of the coast itself. Usually routes are chosen by tour operators to combine a range of different types of coasteering experience.

Vittoriosa, Portomaso and Mġarr have a selection of vessels for rent.

Walking and Hiking
All three islands have many kilometres of country lanes and coastal footpaths that don't require a high fitness level. Because these islands are only small you can appear to cover great distances in a day and it's not easy to get lost. Just remember to come properly equipped with sturdy walking boots. From autumn through to spring, carry a rainproof outer covering and a fleece or warmer layer in case it gets cool. In summer, wear a hat and carry a long-sleeved shirt that can cover your skin against the sun. It's wise to carry sun cream and water at all times of the year.

Kitesurfing
Between October and April the offshore breezes on the northeastern coast are perfect for kitesurfing. There isn't any tuition or equipment rental. Just enjoy the conditions with the local dudes and have a great time.

Kayaking
Taking a kayak trip along the coast offers a totally different view of the Maltese shoreline. Summer is the ideal time, when the water is practically flat and even beginners can enjoy paddling along and looking up at the immense cliffs. Companies offer guided kayak tours, with qualified staff to keep an eye on you.

ONE CHANCE FOR A HOLE IN ONE
The islands have one golf club, The Royal Malta Golf Club at Marsa, close to the capital. Founded by Lieutenant-General Sir Henry D'Oyley Torrens KCB KCMG, who was Malta's Governor at the time, it opened in 1888, and for decades it was a social hub for military types and ex-pats. Today it welcomes guest players with appropriate golf handicaps and you can book multiple rounds at a saving. For details see www.royalmaltagolfclub.com (tel 21223704).

Shopping

Malta has carefully guarded its home-produced handicrafts and these make the best souvenirs of your trip. There is a range of artisan-made items that, for the most part, are pretty light and portable; something that matters a lot in these days of shrinking baggage allowances.

Glass and Silver

The Phoenicians introduced glass blowing to Malta and it remains one of the country's most important crafts, with at least four companies producing ranges. Simply find the style and colour that suits you best. Silver filigree is hand-crafted work produced from thin, featherlight silver wire. Pieces can be as small as a piece of jewellery or as large as a scale model of a sailing *carrack*. The Maltese cross is a popular choice for a souvenir pendant or broach.

Lace

Maltese lace is some of the finest in Europe and has decorated the wardrobes of many European royal houses, but it is expensive. Be aware that mass-produced lace is on sale across the islands, so if you want genuine Maltese lace, buy from a reputable store. You'll also find ceramics in a range of styles.

Edible Souvenirs

The islands have a great range of edible souvenirs (check your country's customs regulations). These include olives and olive oil, capers, sea salt, honey and jams, Gozitan cheese and charcuterie, and quaffable wines.

THE MALTESE CROSS

Found on the national flag, on the rear face of Maltese euro coins, and on the aircraft of Air Malta, the cross is the national symbol of the Maltese nation. It's an eight-pointed star with wide arms and a 'v' at the top of each arm. The symbol became popular during the Crusades, was adopted by the Knights Hospitallers and then carried with them to Malta.

Local crafts of lace making, glass blowing and cheese making provide popular souvenirs and gifts

Malta & Gozo by Night

Malta has two main 'strips' that act as a magnet after dark. The eastern district of Sliema/St. Julian's/Paceville has really developed since the millennium and is the main entertainment hub, for locals as well as visitors. The Buġibba/Qawra/St. Paul's Bay strip is more orientated to the tourist influx. Elsewhere on Malta, and on Gozo too, nightlife is much more low key.

Bars and Clubbing

The capital isn't the place to go for nightlife. Valletta Waterfront, with its restaurants, bars and clubs, is the closest thing to a 'scene', but it's nowhere near as big as Paceville. This vibrant district of open-air bars, eateries and loud clubs is Malta's main fun spot, and open year-round (though in winter it's busiest on Friday and Saturday nights). Nearby St. Julian's is more sophisticated, with cool wine bars playing jazz and New World low-key sounds. The hotels here all have at least one excellent cocktail bar. Meanwhile, the St. Paul's strip appeals to the big-screen sports and karaoke crowd.

Let There Be Light

On Malta and Gozo almost every church and palace is floodlit at night, making Valletta, Vittoriosa, Victoria and Mdina very photogenic.

Bag of Chips?

Malta's casinos open nightly throughout the year. You don't need to be a high roller to enjoy an evening or two here.

For the best nightlife on the islands, head to Paceville with its discos, bars, shows and clubs

---

ARTS AND CULTURE

There's a small but lively cultural scene on the islands. The main season is October to April, with theatrical and orchestral performances at Manoel Theatre and St. James Cavalier Centre for Creativity, and Sagresta Vecchia at Valletta Waterfront. However, there are gallery exhibitions throughout the year, including those at the avant-garde 68 St. Lucy Street (www.68stlucystreet.com). Malta Tourist Authority has information on what's happening (▷ 120).

Eating Out

Maltese cuisine has a small but distinct range of dishes, often based on locally produced or sourced ingredients. Most of the restaurants are based around the capital or around the coast. In the tourist resorts and the major hotels it's possible to eat your way around the world.

Local Cuisine

The influences on Maltese food include Spanish, Moorish and Italian cuisines. Game is popular, the most common being rabbit *(fenek)*, which can be fried or slow-cooked in a rich red wine sauce. Beef olives *(braġjoli)* are thin slices of beef wrapped around a moist filling of breadcrumbs, bacon, eggs and herbs, slow-braised in wine or tomato sauce. Pasta is most authentically served with hearty sauces of liver or rabbit. Of course, on an island, fish and seafood is everywhere, usually simply grilled. Octopus and squid are served in stews.

Snacks

Pastizzi (small filo pastry pasties filled with either ricotta cheese or a pea paste) are an inexpensive (under €1 each) Maltese institution. *Ħobż biż- żejt u it tadem* (bread with oil) is a traditional field-worker/fisherman's lunch. Crusty Maltese bread is rubbed with the inside of a tomato, drizzled in olive oil and then filled with a choice of other items, such as boiled egg or tuna. *Bigilla* is a broad bean paste that's also eaten with bread.

LOCAL TIPPLES

Malta produces an interesting range of drinks. Non-alcoholic effervescent Kinnie is a blend of orange and herbs. The Maltese also mix it with alcohol for unique cocktail recipes. Cisk (pronounced 'Chisk') is Malta's beer. It's a lager style that's been brewed since 1928. The most authentic island wines are by Meridiana, because they grow all their own grapes. Other Maltese companies grow some grapes on the island but import others, usually from Italy. Names to look for are Marsovin and Delicata.

Alfresco and waterside dining is the norm, and fish and seafood lovers won't be disappointed

Restaurants by Cuisine

There are restaurants, cafés, trattorias and bars to suit all tastes and budgets in Malta and Gozo. For a more detailed description of each of our recommendations, see Malta & Gozo by Area.

CAFÉS

Caffe Cordina (▷ 44)
Concept Café (▷ 68)
Fontanella Tea Garden (▷ 90)

CONTEMPORARY/ FUSION

It'Tmun (▷ 106)
Zafiro (▷ 106)

FISH

Café de Paris (▷ 68)
Hunter's Tower (▷ 68)
Ir-Rizzu (▷ 68)
La Vecchia Dogana (▷ 44)

ITALIAN AND PIZZA

CocoPazzo (▷ 44)
Riviera della Marina (▷ 68)
Trattoria AD1530 (▷ 90)
Vecchia Napoli (▷ 90)

MALTESE AND GOZITAN

The Carriage (▷ 44)
Giuseppi's (▷ 90)
Il-Kartell (▷ 106)
Rubino (▷ 44)
Ta'Frenc (▷ 106)
Ta'Kris (▷ 90)
Ta'Rikardu (▷ 106)
Tal-Familja (▷ 68)

MEDITERRANEAN

Blue Creek Bar & Restaurant (▷ 68)
Bonito's (▷ 106)
The Chef (▷ 44)
Country Terrace Lounge Bar & Restaurant (▷ 106)
Madliena Cottage Brasserie (▷ 90)
Malata (▷ 44)
The Medina (▷ 90)

PUB STYLE

Browns (▷ 44)
Café Jubilee (▷ 106)
Fat Harry's (▷ 90)

If You Like...

However you'd like to spend your time in Malta and Gozo, these ideas should help you tailor your perfect visit. Each suggestion has a fuller write-up elsewhere in the book.

BEAUTIFUL BAROQUE

Seek out the facade of the Auberge de Castille et Léon in Valletta (▷ 36).
Admire Preti's fresco cycle on the ceiling of St. John's Co-Cathedral in Valletta, and gaze at Caravaggio's largest canvas, *The Beheading of John the Baptist* (▷ 35).
Wander through St. Paul's Cathedral, in Mdina (▷ 74).

Auberge de Castille et Léon (above top); St. John's Co-Cathedral (above)

PALACES AND MANSIONS

Discover 19th-century entrepreneur style at Palazzo Parisio (▷ 76).
Take in the state rooms and armoury at the Grandmaster's Palace (▷ 30–31).
Learn how the Maltese nobility live at Casa Rocca Piccola (▷ 24).
Appreciate early Siculo-Norman architectural lines at Palazzo Falson (▷ 81).

AN ALFRESCO LUNCH

Find a table overlooking the Gozo Channel at Country Terrace Lounge Bar & Restaurant (▷ 106).
Dine next to the multi-million dollar gin palaces at Riviera della Marina (▷ 68).
Choose a restaurant in the heart of the capital at Malata (▷ 44).
Laze on the waterside at Zafiro (▷ 106).

Independence Square, Rabat (above); Dingli Cliffs (below)

FEELING THE BREEZE

Climb atop Dingli Cliffs (▷ 58).
Walk among the garrigue at Majjistral Nature and History Park (▷ 85).
Relax anywhere on Comino (▷ 96–97).
Explore the backwaters of Delimara Point (▷ 53).

National War Museum
(below)

WORLD WAR II HISTORY

Venture step by step through the conflict at the National War Museum (▷ 38–39).

See how ordinary Maltese built and lived in air-raid shelters at the Malta at War Museum (▷ 62).

Look at the spot where a massive World War II bomb fell through the roof of Mosta Rotunda (▷ 75) in 1942 but failed to explode.

Go back in time to where military decisions were made, at Lascaris War Rooms (▷ 37–38).

SHOPPING FOR SOUVENIRS

Examine unique hand-blown glass objects at Mdina Glass (▷ 88) and Gozo Glass (▷ 104).

Browse handmade Gozitan lace at Bastion Lace (▷ 104).

Check out the delicate and beautiful gold and silver filigree at Joseph Busuttil's (▷ 42) and Stones' (▷ 88).

Add to your cellars by buying a couple of bottles of Meridiana (▷ 14), Marsovin (▷ 66) or Delicata wine.

Ġgantija (above)

Mosta Rotunda (above);
St. Paul's Catacombs (below)

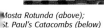

ANCIENT TEMPLES AND CHURCHES

Explore the earliest complex dedicated to the Maltese fertility goddess the Ġgantija temples (▷ 98–99).

Marvel at the Hypogeum (▷ 50–51), said to be the only prehistoric underground temple in the world.

View Byzantine chapels and frescoes at St. Agatha's Catacombs (▷ 77).

Experience St. Paul's Cathedral (▷ 74): a splendid baroque masterpiece.

Wonder at the immense dome of 19th-century Mosta Rotunda (▷ 75).

Pay a visit to 20th-century Ta'Pinu (▷ 101), church of miracles.

CANNON AND MUSKET FIRE

Relive skirmishes between Maltese and French (1798–1800) re-enacted in Alarme! (▷ 37), and inspect the troops of the Knights of St. John during In Guardia! (▷ 43), at Fort St. Elmo.
Feel the weight of Victorian military might at Fort Rinella (▷ 58–59).
Enjoy the showbiz razzmatazz of The Knights Spectacular 1565 (▷ 67).

In Guardia! at Fort St. Elmo (above); Fungus Rock (below); Grand Harbour (bottom)

A BIT OF PAMPERING

Try Malta's first Oxygen Bar at The Athenaeum Spa in the Corinthia Palace Hotel (▷ 112).
Soak up the South East Asian inspired design at Myo Ka Spa at Le Méridien St. Julian's (▷ 112).
Wallow in caviar treatments at The Spa in the Grand Hotel Excelsior (▷ 112).
Unwind looking at magnificent views from the spa at The Radisson Blu Resort (▷ 112).

MESSING ABOUT ON THE WATER

Gaze into the depths of the Blue Lagoon (▷ 97).
Take a trip around the stunning inlet of Grand Harbour (▷ 28–29).
Escape to the uninhabited island of Comino (▷ 96–97).
Sail through the natural arch from the Dwejra Inland Sea to view the Azure Window (▷ 94).

SPOTTING FILM LOCATIONS

The Malta Story (1953)—the true story of Malta's heroic hold-out against Axis forces features Lascaris War Rooms (▷ 37–38), and Grand Harbour (▷ 28–29).
Popeye (1980)—Popeye's Village (▷ 89) was the set from Robert Altman's remake of this cartoon favourite.
Troy (2004)—the Blue Lagoon (▷ 97) features in this epic battle, as Brad Pitt's Achilles fights Eric Bana's Hector.

Malta & Gozo by Area

Valletta

Capital of Malta, Valletta is a UNESCO
World Heritage Site in a stunning setting.

National Museum
of Fine Arts

National Museum of
Archaeology

La Vittoria

Floriana

0		500 metres
0		½ mile

Gozo, Comino

Licata, Pozzalla

Marsamxett Harbour

St Elmo Point (Il-Ponta ta' Sant Iermu)

National War Museum

Fort St Elmo

Catania, Reggio di Calàbria, Salerna

Manoel Theatre

Casa Rocca Piccola

Sacra Infermeria (Mediterranean Conference Centre)

Misrah r-Repubblika

Grandmaster's Palace

VALLETTA

Bibliotheca

Church of St Paul's Shipwreck

St John's Co-Cathedral & Museum

Auberge de Castille et Léon

Grand Harbour

Upper Barrakka Gardens

Lascaris War Rooms

Valletta

H

Casa Rocca Piccola

The Blue Room (left); the Green Room (right)

THE BASICS

www.casaroccapiccola.com

➕ e2

✉ 74 Republic Street

☎ 21221499

🕐 Mon–Sat 10–4

🍴 Restaurant open for lunch Wed–Mon. Also dinner Fri–Sat

♿ None

💷 Moderate

❓ All visits are guided

DID YOU KNOW?

● The 8th Baron and his wife received an invite to the Coronation of Queen Elizabeth II in 1952. While in London they organized a commemorative photo session. The photographer was a young Antony Armstrong-Jones, later to become Earl Snowdon.

Valletta's most important Patrician palazzo adds a wealth of personal detail to the documents and artefacts relating to the history of the Knights Hospitallers and to Malta. It's a window into daily life of days gone by.

The house Built in the 16th century, the house is named after the first owner, Don Pietro La Rocca, who was an Italian admiral of the Knights. The de Piro family bought it in the 18th century and have lived here ever since. The house is replete with furniture, art and collectibles, each with its own story. Generations of the de Piro family look down from hundreds of portraits as you pass from room to room. The *piano nobile* has 12 rooms and beneath the house is a private World War II bomb shelter, converted and expanded from the three wells that used to store water for the house.

The family The de Piro family were members of the Knights of St. John during their time in Rhodes. Cosimo de Piro was made Commander of the Arsenal soon after they arrived on Malta and through the centuries the family were at the right hand of succeeding Grand Masters. The family was rewarded for loyalty with the title Baron of Budach in 1716 and bestowed with the title Marquis de Piro by Philip of Spain in 1742. After the Knights lost control of Malta, the family joined the British and Maltese military or worked in diplomatic and political circles.

The ornate altarpiece (left); highly decorated ceiling (right)

Church of St. Paul's Shipwreck

As the church that celebrates the arrival of St. Paul in unfortunate circumstances, this is one of Malta's most important places of worship. Despite a rather unprepossessing setting, it amply rewards those who venture inside.

The building The exterior is a curious amalgam of differing architectural styles. The original church, erected by Gerolamo Cassar in 1570, was redesigned in 1639 and then again in 1679 to give us the present main structure. It has a 19th-century neo-Gothic facade, designed by Nicola Zammit, that fronts the street and at first glance gives it the look of a bank headquarters, rather than a church.

The interior Francesco Sammut and Lorenzo Gafà designed the interior in 1639, and the riot of baroque detail in this relatively small space is the main feature. The titular gilded wooden statue of St. Paul the Apostle was carved in 1657 by Melchiorre Gafà, brother of Lorenzo. It stands to the left of the main altar, which includes work by Florentine painter Filippo Paladini (1544–1616), one of the most pre-eminent Mannerists to work on Malta and a favourite of Grand Master Verdalle. The church is custodian of several revered relics of St. Paul, including a right wrist bone said to belong to the saint—now housed in an ornate gilded representation of a hand and lower arm—and a fragment of the column on which he was said to have been beheaded.

THE BASICS

+ e3
- 74 St. Paul's Street
- 21236013
- Mon–Sat 8–12, 3–7
- Cafés and restaurants nearby
- None
- Free

HIGHLIGHTS

● Relics of the saint
● 10 February is the saint's feast day, when the statue is paraded through Valletta

ST. PAUL'S SHIPWRECK

Paul was shipwrecked on the island in AD60 on his way to Rome to stand trial for his faith. The Bible tells us that he rid the island of poisonous snakes and his evangelical zeal and healing powers brought about an important convert in the Roman governor Publius. This planted the seeds of Christianity all across the island.

Forts and Fortifications

TOP 25

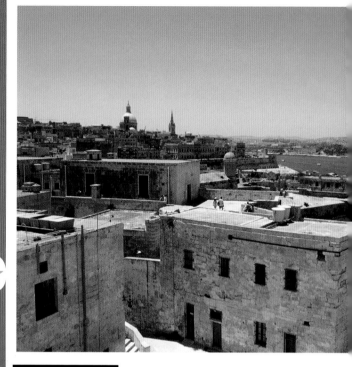

HIGHLIGHTS

● View from Upper Barrakka Gardens (▷ 39) down the line of the Castille Curtain
● Defences around St. James Bastion from the landward side of Triq Gerolamo Cassar

TIP

● The best way to view the fortifications is from beyond the walls of the city. Sliema waterfront or the Three Cities waterfront have good views, but a harbour cruise (▷ 43) gives the best perspective.

The finest citadel in the Mediterranean, Valletta's defences have changed little since they were built at the end of the 16th century. The Hospitallers' architectural legacy remains intact.

History When the Knights Hospitallers arrived on Malta in 1530, they viewed Birgu as a temporary headquarters and commissioned plans for a new city on the better-located Sciberras Peninsula. They hastily erected Fort St. Elmo (▷ 37) to defend the harbour entrance but lack of cash stopped progress. During the Great Siege of 1565, money rolled in from around Europe to defend this front line against the Turks. Military architect Francesco Laparelli arrived in the aftermath of the siege. The green light for his plan came in March

View over Grand Harbour from Fort St. Elmo (left); a corner tower of the 16th-century fortifications around Valletta, with Fort St. Angelo across the harbour (right)

1566. In 1571, with the fortifications almost complete, the Knights Hospitallers moved in.

The Laparelli plan Fort St. Elmo was strengthened but Valletta's most vulnerable flank was landward, so the Laparelli plan called for formidable southwest-facing bastions and two vast cavaliers. Between the two fortifications, curtain walls with small bastions and transverse cuts run down each flank of the city. Within the walls, a grid system of streets made guns, men and horses easy to move around.

Laparelli and Cassar Laparelli died in a plague outbreak in Crete in 1570 but work continued under Maltese engineer Gerolamo Cassar, who is credited with many of the buildings that grace the interior of Valletta.

THE BASICS

➕ f1

✉ Mediterranean Street

🚌 All routes to Valletta

🚢 From Sliema waterfront May–Sep Mon–Sat 7.30, 8, 9, 10 then every 30 min until 6, Sun 7.30, 8, 9, 10 then every 30 min until 4; Oct–Apr Mon–Sat 8, 9, 10 then every 30 min until 5.30, Sun 8, 9, 10, then every 30 min until 3.30. Departures from Valletta back to Sliema are 15 min later than these times

Grand Harbour

TOP 25

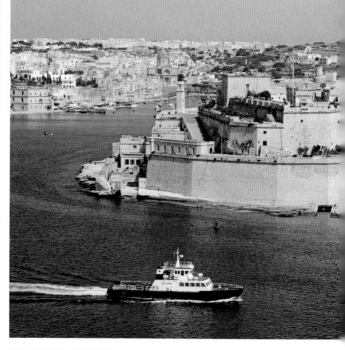

● View across the harbour from Upper Barrakka Gardens (▷ 39)
● The harbour cruise—a sailor's eye view of the harbour and an interesting running commentary (▷ 43)

● The Malta Maritime Museum (▷ 62) is an excellent place for additional information relating to Grand Harbour's form and function through the centuries.

Malta's most emblematic panorama is the vista across Grand Harbour. Made all the better by the magnificent architecture along its shores and the feats of military might, this is one view you can't miss.

Development Sitting in the centre of the Mediterranean, Malta was a strategic island, with the important resource of Grand Harbour's natural safe port. When the Knights arrived in 1530 they fortified the harbour with Fort St. Elmo (▷ 37) on the western mouth, Fort Ricasoli on the opposite mouth, and Fort St. Angelo (▷ 61) in the interior. The Knights transformed the many creeks, including inlets around the Three Cities (▷ 56–57), into dockyards. This kick-started an era of prosperity for the Order, based on international trade. When

A fishing boat sails past Fort St. Angelo on Grand Harbour (left); sightseeing cruise of Grand Harbour (right)

the British took over in 1800, Grand Harbour became the Royal Navy's centre of operations in the Mediterranean, with a home fleet of ships. Malta also serviced and re-stocked trading ships travelling on through the Suez Canal to colonies in India, Singapore and Australia—more than 5,000 of them per year by the end of the 19th century. This was boom time!

Today's activities The baroque warehouses of the old Pinto Wharf, built in 1752, have been renovated and refurbished to create a modern cruise port facility. These leviathan vessels totally dwarf the walls of the fortifications. Not every vessel you see will be a gleaming cruise ship, but something is always chugging by. Look out for the diminutive floatplanes of Harbour Air (▷ 43) too, taking off on regular services.

THE BASICS

➕ e3
✉ Directly east of Valletta
🍴 Cafés and restaurants along Pinto Wharf
🚌 198 from Valletta
🖐 Harbour tours: expensive

Grandmaster's Palace

DID YOU KNOW?

● The Palace Courtyard hosted a meeting between Winston Churchill and Franklin D. Roosevelt in 1945 before they travelled to Yalta for a historic rendezvous with Joseph Stalin to discuss the future of post-war Europe.

TIP

● Check with the tourist office (▷ 120) at the start of your stay to see when the Palace is closed for parliamentary business.

Effectively the headquarters of the Order for nearly 300 years, the Grand Master managed diplomatic and commercial interests from here. Today, it is home to the 69-member Maltese Parliament.

The state rooms The *piano nobile* is the heart of the complex. The Council Chamber, where parliament currently sits, has walls draped with a series of priceless Gobelin tapestries commissioned by Grand Master Ramón Perellos y Rocca. These depict exotic plants and animals captured on newly discovered continents. The Hall of St. Michael and St. George is also known as the Throne Room. There's an excellent 12-cycle frieze depicting the 1565 Siege of Malta by Matteo Perez d'Aleccio (who was a pupil of Michelangelo), and the Minstrel Gallery

Suits of armour on display in the museum of the Grandmaster's Palace (left); the entrance to the palace from Prince Alfred Courtyard (top right); Hall of the Ambassadors (bottom right)

here is the original stern gallery of the carrack *Santa Maria*, one of two ships that originally carried the Knights to Malta. Off here is the State Dining Room, adorned with portraits of British monarchs and impressive 17th-century chandeliers. The Grand Master's Audience Chamber is now the Hall of the Ambassadors. This is also known as the Red Room, because of its crimson walls. Here you'll find a decorative frieze depicting several scenes from the Knights' era on Rhodes.

Palace armoury The armoury is one of the world's finest collections of medieval weapons, with suits of armour and shields, many owned by the Knights. These were wealthy men, so their weapons are of the finest quality, made by the master craftsmen of Europe.

THE BASICS

➕ e2
✉ Palace Square, Republic Street
☎ 21249349
🕐 Armoury: daily 9–5; State Rooms: daily 10–6 (State Rooms may be closed at short notice depending on the parliamentary diary)
🍴 Cafés and restaurants nearby
♿ Few
💷 Expensive
❓ Audioguide €5

National Museum of Archaeology

TOP **25**

Gallery in the museum (left); the Sleeping Lady (right)

THE BASICS

www.heritagemalta.org
🔵 d3
✉ Republic Street
☎ 21556144
🕐 Daily 9–5
🍴 Cafés and restaurants nearby
♿ Few
💷 Moderate

HIGHLIGHTS

● The *Venus of Malta*
● The *Sleeping Lady*
● Original decorations on the temple stone portals
● A model of the Hypogeum

TIPS

● Models or diagrams of the main megalithic sites show the scale of the building works undertaken.
● The 3-D Hypogeum found here is easier to comprehend than on an actual tour of the site.
● A burial site has been re-created with human remains and ritual grave goods.

All the portable finds from the megalithic sites across Malta are on display here. The museum provides excellent background information on the ancient Temple Building civilization.

The building The old Auberge de Provence, built in 1571 and designed by Gerolamo Cassar, was the headquarters of the French-speaking Knights from Provence, one of three *auberges* for French Knights. The other two were lost to damage in World War II.

The collection Although not a huge collection, the displays and items here really do help to piece together what archaeologists know about human development, both in terms of the timescale and innovations. This starts with the early hunter-gatherer Għar Dalam Phase. Exhibits include human remains and tools found at the Għar Dalam site (▷ 59) c.5200–4000BC. The displays and information panels then lead into the important Temple Building era. Archaeologists have divided this into three distinct phases: the Żebbug Phase (4000–3800BC), the Ġgantija Phase (c.3600–3000BC) and the Tarxien Phase (3000–2500BC). For each phase, the locations are discussed and finds are displayed, including the original deco-rated temple portals and the exquisite rounded female figurines; the most important finds of this fertility cult. The *Venus of Malta,* discovered at Ħaġar Qim (▷ 49), and the *Sleeping Lady,* found in the Hypogeum (▷ 50–51), are best.

Part of the collection (left); 18th-century staircase (right)

National Museum of Fine Arts

Malta's flagship art museum can't match the Louvre or the Uffizi, but it has several pieces of international acclaim and strong displays of renowned artists with a particular connection to Malta.

Architecture Built as a private palazzo, the building was remodelled in the 1760s by a Portuguese Knight of the Order, who installed the magnificent marble staircase. During the British era it was the seat of the Commander in Chief of the Mediterranean Fleet.

The collections There are 30 gallery rooms in total and much of the collection has a connection with the Knights. The museum holds a large number of works by Mattia Preti (rooms 12 and 13) including an impressive *Martyrdom of St. Catherine of Alexandria*, displayed immediately at the top of the staircase to the *piano nobile*. Antoine de Favray (1706–92) also has his own room (14), where a series of likenesses of Grand Masters are on view. Many of the artists may not be of international renown, but the collection of works depicting Malta through the centuries is fascinating. From bucolic island scenes to naval panoramas, it's a chance to see how the island and its landmarks have changed. The prized piece is a scene by J. M. W. Turner (1775–1851). Author and poet Edward Lear (1812–88) was inspired to draw and paint a whole range of scenes, and Grand Harbour is the subject of several large canvasses by Louis Ducros (1748–1810).

THE BASICS

www.heritagemalta.org
- c2
- South Street
- 22954341
- Daily 9–5
- Cafés and restaurants nearby
- Few
- Moderate. Combined ticket: expensive

DID YOU KNOW?

● Mattia Preti (1613–99) painted the major corpus of his work on Malta, which can be found in churches and collections across the island. Born in Taverna in Calabria, he was apprenticed to a painter of the Caravaggio school and was influenced by the artist's style. Appointed a Knight of St. John in 1642, he first visited the headquarters in Malta in 1659. He returned again in 1661 and stayed until his death.

Sacra Infermeria

A hall displaying Knights Hospitallers banners (left); entrance door (right)

THE BASICS

www.mcc.com.mt

🕂 f2

✉ Mediterranean Street

☎ 21243840

🕓 Mon–Fri 9.30–4.30, Sat–Sun 9.30–4

🍴 Café at the bastion (€)

🚌 198

♿ Good

👑 Moderate

HIGHLIGHTS

● The Great Ward
● The Knights Hospitallers walk-through exhibition
● The Malta Experience audiovisual attraction (▷ 43)

If any one building epitomizes the *raison d'être* of the Knights of St. John, it's this limestone edifice that dominates the northeastern quadrant of the city. This was the state-of-the-art medical facility of the late medieval period.

Origins Throughout the Crusades in the Holy Land, the Knights tended pilgrims with their legendary medical skills. When they arrived in Malta they continued this service and built the Sacra Infermeria (Holy Infirmary or Holy Hospital). Started in 1574, the hospital reached its current size in the 1660s. The cathedral-like Great Ward was one of the largest covered spaces in Europe at the time. Almost 1,000 patients could be treated here. The Knights Hospitallers walk-through exhibition in the Magazine Ward re-creates a ward from this era, and explains the history of the Order. Nicolas Cotoner founded a School of Anatomy and Surgery at the hospital in 1676. Under British rule it continued to conduct medical research and David Bruce made the discovery of brucellosis (undulant fever germ) here in 1887.

Recent history Throughout the 19th and early 20th centuries, the hospital cared for hundreds of British and Commonwealth soldiers but it was closed after World War I and subsequently used as the police headquarters. The hospital was damaged during World War II and fell into decline until it was fully restored and opened as the Mediterranean Conference Centre in 1979.

Barrel-vaulted baroque ceiling (left); The Beheading of John the Baptist *(right)*

St. John's Co-Cathedral & Museum

No expense was spared by the Knights in the decorative detail in this cathedral, and in the numerous ornate tombs of the Grand Masters buried here.

The cathedral Designed by Gerolamo Cassar and completed in 1577, the rather fortress-like exterior is one of the few Mannerist facades in the city. The interior has a riot of complex decoration, from frescoes and finely carved stone panels to gilded stucco and wood. Side chapels branch out from the nave, and each is dedicated to a different *langue* (division of knights). Mattia Preti was commissioned to decorate many elements of the cathedral, including a fresco cycle depicting the life of John the Baptist on 18 panels of the cathedral ceiling. Eleven early Grand Masters are buried in the crypt. Later Grand Masters lie in elaborate tombs in the main body of the church and the ornate tombstones of more than 400 ordinary knights are set into the cathedral floor.

The oratory Caravaggio's only signed canvas and his largest work, *The Beheading of John the Baptist* (1608), dominates this room.

Museum The cathedral museum holds a vast collection of ecclesiastical treasures, including vestments of cloth woven with gold and silver, jewel encrusted goblets, and a priceless set of monumental Flemish tapestries. The chair used by Pope John Paul II during his visit to Malta in 1990 is on display.

THE BASICS

www.stjohnscocathedral.com
🔲 d3
✉ St. John's Square (visitor entrance on Republic Street)
☎ 21220536
🕐 Mon–Fri 9.30–4.30, Sat 9.30–12.30
🍴 Cafés and restaurants nearby
♿ Good
💷 Moderate
❓ The entrance fee includes an audioguide (multi-language). Visitor numbers will be limited

HIGHLIGHTS

● Beheading of St. John painting by Caravaggio
● Ornate floor made of tombstones of the Knights
● Tombs of the Grand Masters in the crypt

TIP

● Every chapel, tomb and painting has a tale to tell here. Make sure you pick up an audioguide.

VALLETTA
TOP 25

35

More to See

AUBERGE DE CASTILLE ET LÉON

Each of the divisions, or *langues,* of the Knights Hospitallers constructed an inn, or *auberge,* as their headquarters and social centre. The Auberge de Castille et Léon accommodated knights hailing from Castille, Léon (both now part of Spain) and Portugal. The original and extensive *auberge*, probably designed by Gerolamo Cassar in 1574, has been remodelled and embellished with a magnificent baroque facade (1741), which is one of the finest in the city. An army headquarters during the British era, the *auberge* became home to the offices of the Prime Minister following independence.
✚ d3 ⊠ Castille Square ⊙ Not open to the public ⅍ None

BIBLIOTHECA

www.libraries-archives.gov.mt
Grand Master Claude de la Sengle was the first to suggest a library for the archives of the Order. However, this purpose-built library was not completed until 1796, only two years before the Knights were ousted. Today, as Malta's National Library, it holds a vast archive of information about the Knights Hospitallers and their business, from before their time on Malta to the takeover by the French. The oldest document is a charter by King Baldwin I of Jerusalem dating from 1107. The library also holds a collection of *melitensia*; works by Maltese authors or works about the Maltese islands by foreign authors.
✚ d2 ⊠ Misrah Ir-Repubblika (Republic Square) ☎ 21236585 ⊙ 16 Jun–30 Sep Mon–Fri 8.30–1.15, Sat 8.15–1; 1 Oct–15 Jun Mon–Fri 8.30–5.45, Sat 8.15–1 ⅍ None 🍴 Free; ID needed for entry

FLORIANA

The original footprint of Valletta eventually became overcrowded and a suburb, Floriana, was built inland with a further line of formidable defences at the landward boundary. Named after architect

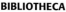
Auberge de Castille et Léon and gardens

Statue in Maglio Gardens in Floriana

Pietro Floriani, the city is characterized by fine patrician mansions and handsome offices and apartments. The architecture works as a unified whole—a triumph of town planning—though the district now has a rather careworn patina and is in need of some renovation. Below ground there are vast granaries, built to guard provisions against any long-term sieges and last used in World War II. Argotti Botanical Gardens (at St. Phillip's Bastion), laid out in the 18th century as a private garden of Grand Master Pinto, are the main attractions in the district. The major church is the St. Publius, inaugurated in 1792.

🔲 b4 ✉ South of Valletta beyond the landward bastions 🍴 Cafés/bars 🚌 All routes to the Valletta terminus 🦽 Few

FORT ST. ELMO

The headland of the Sciberras peninsula, guarding the mouths of both Grand Harbour (▷ 28–29) and Marsamxett Harbour, was first fortified by the Knights in 1552,

and this first Fort St. Elmo, an isolated defensive position, held out for 30 days before being overrun by the Ottomans during the Great Siege. When Valletta was built, Fort St. Elmo was integrated into the wider defensive plan (▷ 26–27) and strengthened to become a formidable fort. It remained in military use until after World War II and today houses the Maltese Police Academy and the National War Museum (▷ 38–39). The military re-enactments In Guardia! (▷ 43) and Alarme! are held within the fort complex.

🔲 f1 ✉ Mediterranean Street ⏰ Not open to the public except for National War Museum (▷ 38–39), and In Guardia! and Alarm! (▷ 43) 🚌 98

LASCARIS WAR ROOMS

www.wirtartna.org

Set deep in the defensive walls surrounding Valletta, the War Rooms became headquarters to military operations during the Battle of Malta (1940–43). Impervious to

The colourful In Guardia! parade at Fort St. Elmo

the bombs dropped by Axis forces, the rooms operated 24 hours a day to monitor enemy movements, plan allied actions and maintain contact with London. The vast complex is gradually being renovated by Fondazzjoni Wirt Artna (the Malta Heritage Trust) and the rooms that are open to the public are authentic in every detail.

➕ d4 ✉ Lascaris Ditch ☎ 21234717 🕐 Daily 10–5 ♿ Few 💵 Expensive

MANOEL THEATRE

www.teatrumanoel.com.mt

The theatre was personally funded by Grand Master António Manoel de Vilhena and opened in 1732. Performances were originally organized by a knight called 'Il Protettore', but the responsibility for this later passed to a commercial impresario. Fully restored in 1960, the semi-circular house glisters like new and has wonderful acoustics. The theatre now plays host to a full schedule of performances of dance, drama, opera and musicals, as well as concerts, recitals and the visual arts, between October and May.

➕ d2 ✉ 115, Old Theatre Street ☎ 21246389 🕐 Guided tours: Mon–Fri 10.15, 11, 11.45, 12.30, 1.15, 2, 2.45, 3.30; Sat 10.15, 11, 11.45, 12.30 🍴 Café (€) ♿ Few 💵 Inexpensive

MISRAH IR-REPUBBLIKA

The small Republic Square, flanked by the Grandmaster's Palace (▷ 30–31) and the Bibliotheca (▷ 36), is the social heart of Valletta. In the British era it was called Queen's Square and a statue of Victoria still stands here; notice her fine shawl, which is made of Gozo lace. Filled with the tables of several cafés, including Cordina (▷ 44), it's the place to stop for a drink and watch the world go by.

➕ d2 ✉ Republic Street 🍴 Cafés ♿ None

NATIONAL WAR MUSEUM

www.heritagemalta.org

A wealth of genuine artefacts is the anchor to this comprehensive museum relating to Malta's

The Manoel Theatre, beautifully restored in 1960 to its 18th-century glory

involvement in the conflicts of the 20th century. These are complemented by a fascinating oral soundtrack, letters and photographs. These add a wealth of detail to pivotal moments during World War II, such as the Siege of Malta, Operation Pedestal—the convoy that kept the island from running out of food and fuel—and the background to Malta being awarded the George Cross in 1942.

➕ e1 ✉ Fort St. Elmo, Mediterranean Street ☎ 21222430 🕐 Daily 8.15–5 ♿ Good ✋ Moderate

UPPER BARRAKKA GARDENS

The private gardens of the Italian Auberge from 1661, the greenery now offers a shady place for Valletta residents to come and relax. Set on the upper ramparts of the city walls, the gardens offer superb views across Grand Harbour (▷ 28–29) and the Three Cities (▷ 56–57). A noonday gun is fired from the Gun Saluting Battery (for more information see www.wirtartna.org),

just below the terrace of the gardens, as it has been for centuries. Before the era of pocket watches the firing signalled the middle of the day to allow synchronization of ships' chronographs across the whole harbour.

➕ d4 ✉ Castille Place 🕐 Open access 🍴 Outdoor café (€) ♿ None ✋ Free

LA VITTORIA

Named Church of Our Lady of Victories, to commemorate the military victory of the Knights over the Ottoman forces, this tiny church was the first place of worship completed in Valletta. Grand Master de la Valette was laid to rest here after his death in 1568, until his body was transferred to St. John's Co-Cathedral. The bust on the facade is that of Pope Innocent XII, who had been an Inquisitor stationed in Malta.

➕ d3 ✉ Ordnance Street ☎ 21245680 🕐 Irregular hours (phone in advance) ♿ None ✋ Free

Elegant Italianate Upper Barrakka Gardens

Around Valletta

This short walk in Valletta allows you to enjoy a range of attractions in the upper town, with plenty of cafés and shops on the way.

DISTANCE: 1km (0.6 miles) **ALLOW:** 2–4 hours with stops

START

CITY GATE
➕ c3 🚌 All services to Valletta

❶ Cross City Gate to Republic Street. Walk 100m (110 yards) and turn right immediately after the remains of the Opera House (the building site for the new Parliament building).

❷ Follow the road around to Castille Square, with the Auberge de Castille et Léon (▷ 36) on your left.

❸ Carry on in the same direction and cross the top of St. Paul's Street (which starts on your left). Keep the Castille Hotel on your left and walk to Upper Barrakka Gardens (▷ 39) for views across Grand Harbour (▷ 28–29).

❹ Retrace your steps to St. Paul's Street and turn right. After three blocks (around 5 minutes' walk) the Church of St. Paul's Shipwreck (▷ 25) sits on the left.

END

ST. GEORGE'S SQUARE
➕ d2 🚌 All services to Valletta

❽ Continue down Republic Street to Republic Square (▷ 38). Beyond this small square is St. George's Square, with the Grandmaster's Palace (▷ 30–31) on your right.

❼ Walk straight ahead past the entrance to reach Republic Street and turn right. This major conduit through the city is always busy. The visitor entrance to St. John's Co-Cathedral is 50m (55 yards) down on the right.

❻ Turn left here and then right at the next intersection, to enter St. John's Street. St. John's Co-Cathedral (▷ 35) is on the right.

❺ After visiting the church take the narrow road to the west (up the hill), Santa Lucija, and walk to the next intersection, Merchant's Street.

Shopping

CAFFE CORDINA

www.caffecordina.com

You can buy a range of beautifully packaged, tempting edibles here, made on the premises. Maltese nougat and honey rings are the most popular choices. Try cheese and honey sourced from farms on Gozo. There's also a shop in the airport if you'd rather buy just before you fly.

🔳 d2 ✉ 244 Republic Street
☎ 21234385

CASA ROCCA PICCOLA

www.casaroccapiccola.com

The current owner of the Casa (▷ 24) is a prolific author on various aspects of Malta history and, in addition to a variety of the usual souvenirs, stocks his own books and an interesting and extensive range of others about the island.

🔳 e2 ✉ 74 Republic Street
☎ 21221499

C. GALEA PAINTINGS

This gallery sells a range of art, some with island themes. They may be more expensive than the average souvenirs but you will certainly have unique views of your trip.

🔳 d3 ✉ 8 Merchants Street
☎ 21243591

JOSEPH BUSUTTIL

This tiny family-owned shop sells a range of handmade silver filigree and Maltese lace. They also stock a small selection of Maltese glass. It's an excellent option for quality souvenirs in the city.

🔳 d3 ✉ 222 Merchants Street ☎ 21243241

MALTA CRAFT CENTRE

You'll find only Maltese and Gozitan-produced crafts here but it's an eclectic range and not a very extensive one. Handmade cotton rugs and textiles are both inexpensive and practical souvenirs, and you won't be able to find these in many other outlets.

🔳 d3 ✉ 9–10 Freedom Square ☎ 21223660

PEDIGREE TOYSHOPS

A range of well-made, quality souvenirs suitable for children is on sale at this toyshop. You will also find items with a particular Maltese theme,

---

CLOSING DAY

Don't forget that, even though Malta is busy summer tourist destination, most shops in Valletta and the non-tourist towns will be closed on Sundays. Those that do open tend to open in the morning only, leaving the streets eerily quiet. On the plus side, though, this is a great time to wander the streets and alleyways to take in the wealth of fine architectural gems.

---

including some lovely glass and lace.

🔳 c5 ✉ Pinto Wharf, Valletta Waterfront ☎ 21226800

R. GRECH JEWELLERS

This is a family-owned jewellery workshop and retail shop, so you are welcome to watch the artisans at work creating pieces, then browse the range of silver and gold items on sale. There's a stock of filigree, and pieces in gold and silver set with attractive semi-precious stones.

🔳 e2 ✉ 69 Republic Street
☎ 21236805

STERLING

There's a good range of gemstones, watches and fashion jewellery on sale at this chic emporium, which also has a branch at Sliema.

🔳 c5 ✉ Pinto Wharf, Valletta Waterfront
☎ 21221932

SUNDAY FLEA MARKET

The biggest market on the island is held every Sunday morning. There are bric-à-brac cum antique stalls, where you may find a one-of-a-kind souvenir from the island. These include old photographs and lace items, but stalls also sell mass-produced products galore. You can haggle a little for the price of T-shirts or beach towels. There is a caged wild bird section.

🔳 c3 ✉ St. James Ditch

Entertainment and Activities

CAPTAIN MORGAN CRUISES

www.captainmorgan.com.mt
Enjoy a tour of the Grand Harbour with an informative commentary. This is the best way to get a view of the fortifications of Valletta and Grand Harbour. Departures are from the ferry dock in Sliema (▷ 78).

🔒 d2 ✉ Tigne Seafront, Sliema Harbour ☎ 23463333 🕐 May–Sep daily 10, 11, 12.15, 1.15, 2.45 (Jun–Sep also 3.30 if sufficient demand); Oct–Apr daily 10.30, 12.30, 2.45 (also 11.30, 1.15 if sufficient demand) 🚌 62 (night service), 64, 66, 67, 68, 662, 667, 671 from Valletta; 65 from Mdina/Rabat; 645, 652 from Ċirkewwa; 627 from The Three Cities/Marsaxlokk; 49 (night service) from Mosta ⛴ Ferry to Valletta

CITY AUDIO TOUR

www.myguide.com.mt
This self-guided tour with multi-language handset helps you get the best out of a stroll around the streets of Valletta.

🔒 d3 and e2 ✉ Handsets from: National Museum of Archaeology (▷ 32); Grandmaster's Palace (▷ 30–31) ☎ 21221628 🕐 National Museum of Archaeology: daily 9–7; Grandmaster's Palace: daily 9–5

HARBOUR AIR

www.harbourairmalta.com
The Harbour Air floatplanes take off on the water of Grand Harbour and carry you on an amazing scenic low-level tour of Malta and Gozo. It's a fantastic trip.

🔒 c5 ✉ Upper Wharf, Pinto Wharf, Valletta Waterfront ☎ 21228302 🕐 Several flights daily, weather permitting 🚌 198

IN GUARDIA!

Stand Guard!—for a full-on re-enactment of a Hospitallers' military parade in the heart of one of their most formidable fortresses, Fort St. Elmo (▷ 37). Watch the Grand Master inspect his troops and assess their readiness for battle.

🔒 f1 ✉ Fort St. Elmo, Mediterranean Street ☎ 22915400 🕐 Sep–Jun most Sundays 11am 🚌 198

THE KNIGHTS HOSPITALLERS

www.knightshospitallers.com
This walk-through experience presents dioramas depicting the Knights and the major events in their tenure of Malta.

🔒 f2 ✉ Mediterranean Conference Centre, Mediterranean Street ☎ 21243840 🕐 Mon–Fri 9.30–4.30, Sat–Sun 9.30–4 🚌 198

THE MALTA EXPERIENCE

www.themaltaexperience.com
This impressive audio-visual extravaganza takes you on a tour through the 7,000 years of Malta's history. The film also shows the stunning landscapes of the island.

🔒 f2 ✉ St. Elmo Bastions, Mediterranean Street ☎ 21243776 🕐 Mon–Fri 11, 12, 1, 2, 3, 4; Sat–Sun 11, 12, 1 (also Jun–Oct Sat–Sun 2pm) 🚌 198

MANOEL THEATRE

www.teatrumanoel.com.mt
Events at this historic theatre run the whole gamut from international opera to gospel music.

🔒 d2 ✉ 115 Old Theatre Street ☎ 21246389 🕐 Sep–May

ST. JAMES CAVALIER CENTRE FOR CREATIVITY

www.sjcav.org
A vibrant centre for contemporary art combines galleries, cinema screens and stages for live performances, all set in the historic St. James Cavalier.

🔒 d3 ✉ Castille Square ☎ Box office: 21223200 🕐 Mon–Tue 9–5, Thu–Fri 9–9, Sat–Sun 10–9

A NEW VENUE

Malta's popular Opera House was bombed and badly damaged in World War II. For almost 60 years the location just inside the city gate remained a glaring scar on the cityscape, but in 2010 work finally began on a regeneration of the site; not an opera House but a new Parliament building and an open-air performance venue. Designed by Renzo Piano, it should be complete in 2016.

VALLETTA

ENTERTAINMENT AND ACTIVITIES

Restaurants

PRICES

Prices are approximate, based on a 3-course meal for one person.
€€€   over €30
€€   €20–€30
€   under €20

BROWNS (€–€€)

www.brownsmalta.com
This pub-style eatery with a terrace, on Pinto Wharf, specializes in aged Angus steaks but also serves ribs and pies. Browns transforms into a club as evening turns to night.
➕ c5 ✉ Valletta Waterfront ☎ 21227410 🕐 Daily breakfast, lunch and dinner 🚌 198

CAFFE CORDINA (€)

www.caffecordina.com
The place to come to watch the world go by at a table in Republic Square. Caffé Cordina is famous for its cakes but also has a good range of lunch snacks.
➕ d2 ✉ 244 Republic Street (at Republic Square) ☎ 21234385 🕐 Daily breakfast and lunch

THE CARRIAGE (€€€)

A long-standing favourite with locals and visitors for a relaxed alfresco lunch, The Carriage offers a limited but delicious seasonal menu. The main attraction is the view of the city from the terrace.
➕ d2 ✉ Valletta Buildings, South Street ☎ 21247828 🕐 Mon–Fri lunch, Sat lunch and dinner

THE CHEF (€€–€€€)

This chef, Martin Camilleri has created award-winning cuisine for the leading hotels on Malta. His own muse is to concentrate on slow food, and his daily specials are to be recommended.
➕ c3 ✉ Windmill Street ☎ 21250837 🕐 Mon–Fri lunch and dinner, Sat dinner

COCOPAZZO (€)

A good value, relaxed place for lunch, serving fresh fish, pizzas and pasta that's made to order. You'll share the dining room with the locals; always a good sign.
➕ d2 ✉ Valletta Buildings, South Street ☎ 21235706 🕐 Daily lunch and dinner

MALATA (€€)

www.malatamalta.com
This small basement bistro is the perfect setting for an intimate eatery and

MALTA KULINARJA

Competition between the chefs of the best hotels and restaurants on the island is fierce and it is important to keep skills honed in this very competitive tourist market. In 2009 the Malta Chefs' Society, the Malta Cookery and Food Association and the Malta Culinary Association got together to launch a new initiative, Malta Kulinarja, to see just who is the best. It's an annual event held in November.

has a terrace on Palace Square. The menu swings between French and Maltese. Enjoy live jazz every Tuesday and Friday evening.
➕ d2 ✉ Palace Square ☎ 21233967 🕐 Mon–Sat lunch and dinner, (Sun lunch winter only)

RUBINO (€€€)

www.giuseppismalta.com
Rubino's brings back the dishes mama used to make. There's no menu but everything that's prepared in the kitchen is seasonal, fresh and delicious, with the emphasis on traditional Maltese recipes. Tagliata is prime grilled beef with parmesan shavings.
➕ e2 ✉ Old Bakery Street ☎ 21224656 🕐 Mon–Fri lunch, Tue, Thu–Sat for dinner, Sun am for coffee and pastries

LA VECCHIA DOGANA (€€–€€€)

www.lavecchiadogana.com
On elegant Floriana's western flank, the Old Customs House—as the restaurant is known in English—imaginatively fits an ultra contemporary interior into one of Malta's historic buildings. The innovative menu concentrates on seafood but also serves an excellent *bistecca alla Fiorentina* (an Italian porterhouse or T-bone steak)
➕ H6 ✉ Sa Maison, Pieta ☎ 21226662 🕐 Tue–Sun lunch and dinner 🚌 62, 66 from Valletta/Sliema

The South

Much of Malta's modern commercial infrastructure is found in the south of the island, but there are pretty fishing harbours and miles of rugged cliffs to enjoy. History has dealt a good hand too, with ancient temples, baroque palaces, and the Three Cities with their superb museums to visit.

3

4

5

6

7
Dingli
Hal-Tartarni
Tal-Vecca
Dingli Cliffs
Buskett
Verdala Palace
Buskett Gardens
Ta' Rapa
Ghajn Il-Kbira
Il-Hamrija
Clapham Junction
257
Ta' Dmejrek
Siggiewi
Ta' L-Ghaqba
Hal-Farru
Ta' Kircippu
Kandja

8
Gebel Cantar
Tal-Lewza
Ta' Hax-Xlug
Tal-Providenza
Tal-Lanza
Dar tal-Providenza
Ghar Lapsi
Hagar Qim
Mnajdra
Qrendi
Tal-Fulija
Ta' Hal-Lew
In-Nigret
Mqabba
Tal-Mentna
Tal-Bebb
Zurri
Wied Ful
Blue Grotto

9

10
0   3 km
0   2 miles

C   D   E   F

Gozo, Comino

Licata, Portalla

Catania, Réggio di Calábria, Salerno

Ricasoli Point
(Il-Ponta ta' Ricasoli)

Fort St Angelo
Vittoriosa
Rinella
Fort Rinella
Kalkara
Santu Rokku
Ras il-Gebel
Senglea
Maritime Museum
Inquisitor's Palace
Xghajra
St Joseph's Oratory
Malta at War Museum
Il-Hofra
San Leonardu
Kordin
Cospicua
Marsa
Paola
Fgura
Zabbar
Imgieret
Bulebel iz-Zghir
Zonqor
Hypogeum
Tarxien Temples
Tarxien
Santa Lucija
Marsaskala
Ta' Latnija
Il-Kappara
iqa
Bulebel il-Kbir
Il-Minzel
Ta' Ngraw
Tas-Sienja
Tal-Faqqani
Gebel ta' San Martin
-Wilga
Tal-Mithna
Ta' San Girgor
St Thomas' Bay
(Il-Bajja ta' San Tumas)
9
Ghaxaq
Zejtun
Misrah Strejnu
Ta' Lombardi
Gudja
Ta' Garda
Ta' Hal-Ginwi
30
Kirkop
Bur Maghtab
Marsaxlokk
Tas-Slig
Xrobb I-Ghagin
Il-Karwija
Hofra Il-Kbira
Safi
Ghar Dalam
Il-Biex
Ras il-Fenek
Ta' Amparell
Il-Fiddin
Ta' Germun
Il-Qajjenza
Peter's Pool
baqra
Tumbrell
Tumbrell Point
(Il-Ponta tat-Tumbrell)
Ta' Ghammer
Birzebbuga
Marsaxlokk Bay
(Il-Bajja ta' Marsaxlokk)
Delimara
Ta' Salvun
Pretty Bay
(Il-Bajja ta' Birzebbuga)
Il-Mizieb
Ta'-Papa
Delimara Point
(Il-Ponta ta' Delimara)
Hal-Far
Kalafrana
Benghajsa
Il-Ponta ta' Benghajsa

G   H   J   K

Blue Grotto

TOP
25

A small tour boat enters the grotto (left); sculpted cliffs enclose the grotto (right)

Considered one of Malta's premier natural attractions, the Blue Grotto satisfies our desire for dramatic beautiful landscapes. It could tell us a lot about the geological antecedents of the island if we weren't so distracted by the view.

Spectacular geology Malta's south and west coast is characterized by cliffs hewn by the power of nature, but this one feature has captured the public imagination. Named the Blue Grotto by the British, in Maltese it is known as Il-Hnejja or The Arch. It was formed by natural erosion of wind and waves to create a large, natural overhang supported by a tall, slim pedestal of rock. Enter through the arch to view the six caves in the connecting system. The water here is calm, crystal clear and brilliant azure, due to the sunlight reflecting off the white sand below. You'll be able to spot the occasional fish, or more likely a scuba diver.

Boat trips Boats set sail from the tiny inlet of Wied iż-Żurrieq, just to the west. These traditional *luzzu* craft are gaily painted in traditional yellows and powder blue, with the eye symbol at the prow to ward off evil. Early in the morning is the best time to visit in the summer. The sun enters the furthest reaches of the caverns at this time, the sea is calmest and the crowds haven't yet arrived. If you don't want to take the boat trip, or the weather isn't conducive, there's a viewing platform just west of the grotto that has a spectacular view of the arch.

Ħaġar Qim & Mnajdra

The largest monolith towers above standing stones (left); the path leading to the complex (right)

The most dramatic of all Malta's megalithic temples, Ħaġar Qim sits high on a windswept hill with views down to the Mediterranean Sea. It's perhaps here that you can really appreciate the skills of the Temple Builders, and their enduring relationship with nature and the passing seasons.

Ħaġar Qim First excavated in 1839 and dating from the Ġgantija phase (c.3600–3200BC), this is a single temple unit, but ancient remains close by lead archaeologists to postulate that it may once have been part of a larger complex. Within the structure there are several chambers surrounded by an enclosure of standing stones, the largest measuring 6.4m (21ft) and weighing in the region of 20 tonnes. Finds at Ħaġar Qim (the name means 'Standing Stones') have added a great deal to what little archaeologists know about the Temple Builders. A decorative pillar altar, two table altars and collections of Rubenesque statues of fertility goddesses or priestesses, have all been found here.

Mnajdra Tucked away against the hillside below Ħaġar Qim, Mnajdra is a complex of three temples leading off an oval forecourt. The oldest temple dates from the same time as Ħaġar Qim. However, the third temple is younger, dating from the Tarxien period (3000–2500BC) and is especially noteworthy because its finely worked facade of coralline limestone has survived relatively undamaged by the ravages of time.

THE BASICS

www.heritagemalta.org
✚ F8 and E8
✉ Triq Ħaġar Qim, 2km (1.2 miles) from Qrendi
☎ 21424231
🕐 Daily 9–5
🍴 Café
🚌 38, 138 from Valletta
♿ Visitor centre: good; site: few
💰 Expensive

DID YOU KNOW?

● In 2009, both temples were fitted with high-tech canopies to protect them from the elements. It's a controversial move and affects the aesthetics. These covers are temporary structures, however, and can be removed without harm to the temples.

TIP

● Copies of the decorative stonework lie in situ; the originals and statues are at the National Museum of Archaeology (▷ 32).

Hypogeum

TOP
25

HIGHLIGHTS

● The sheer complexity of the structure, carved with non-metal hand tools
● The Oracle's architecture
● Red ochre wall decoration

TIPS

● You can't take anything into the Hypogeum, so keep valuables on your person.
● The model of the *Sleeping Lady* at the site is a copy. The original is in the National Museum of Archaeology (▷ 32) in Valletta.

This ancient complex of temple and catacombs is unique within Europe. It is a fascinating insight into the technical skills of the Temple Building peoples, and their preoccupations with their place in this world, and the world beyond.

Background A 15-minute film sets the scene and gives excellent background to the people who created the Hypogeum and how they achieved this incredible feat; a complex that extends to 500sq m (5,380sq ft), carved only with bone tools. The Hypogeum was in use for more than 1,000 years and has three levels: the upper level, the oldest at c.3600BC–2200BC, the middle level c.3300BC–3000BC and the lowest level, 10.6m (34.8ft) below ground, which was in use c.3150BC–2500BC.

The main hall of the temple, hollowed out of limestone around 4,500 years ago (left); decorated ceiling of the Oracle Chamber (right)

Burial practice Bodies decomposed in chambers at ground level and then the bones were interred in underground chambers. Once interred, the bones were never removed. As a chamber became filled with bones, another chamber would be carved and the bones of the full chamber would be covered in soil to create a floor level. The bones of more than 7,000 individuals were found here. Many were daubed in red ochre, which also decorates the walls. The Oracle Chamber, or inner sanctum—the deepest point in the structure—has a finely worked ceiling and shows an appreciation of architectural lines. Objects found include bowls, pendants, needles and axe heads, many of which are on display at the site. The *Sleeping Lady*, an exquisite miniature statue of a round-bodied female, was found here in 1905.

THE BASICS

www.heritagemalta.org
➕ H7
✉ Burial Street, Paula
☎ 21805018
🕐 Daily; tours on the hour 9–4. Book in advance on the website
🚌 11 to the Hypogeum from Valletta, 8, 12, 27, 29, 30 115 to nearby
♿ Good
💰 Expensive
❓ No admittance to children under 6

Marsaskala

HIGHLIGHTS

- The pretty, sheltered waterfront
- Relaxed atmosphere
- The natural playgrounds just to the south

TIPS

- Marsaskala offers a good range of restaurants and bars, and one club. If you want wilder nights, head to St. Julian's/Paceville (▷ 83).
- St. Peter's Pool, off the coast, is one of Malta's top dive sites.

The largest resort east of Valletta, Marsaskala has a slight air of yesteryear compared with the modern waterfront of St. Julian's, and that's no bad thing. It is a place to slow down, relax and really get into the pace of island life.

The harbour The natural inlet, with its slight bend, offers a particularly sheltered harbour that can't be seen from the open sea. This is a blessing for native shipping but can be a curse, such as when the Turks used this natural advantage and laid their naval ships low here during their final attempt to take Malta in 1614. However, although the Ottoman troops reached the shore, they were beaten in a land battle and the Knights built a *fortizza* on the high ground to plug the gap in their defences.

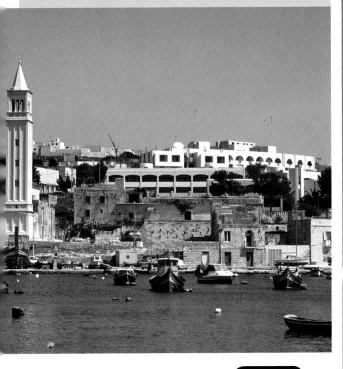

The waterfront (left); fishing boats moored in Marsaskala harbour, overlooked by St. Thomas Tower (right)

The town Tourism has developed quickly around the dramatic headlands—including a huge number of houses and apartments only used in summer—but it hasn't overtaken the essentially local character of the town and this is its charm. People sit at cafés chatting over a glass or two of Cisk; no one seems to be in a great rush to get anywhere.

The headlands Running south to Marsaxlokk (▷ 60) and incorporating the sweeping St. Thomas' Bay, Xrobb I-Ghagin and the Delimara Point, the headlands could be the location of Malta's next National Park. It is certainly splendid enough and an excellent playground for walkers and cyclists on land, and divers and kayakers offshore. Some of Malta's most challenging and dramatic dive sites lie off this stretch of coast.

THE BASICS

🔁 K7
✉ 9km (5.5 miles) south-east of Valletta
🍴 Cafés and restaurants
🚌 18, 19, 20, 21, 22 from Valletta

53

Tarxien Temples

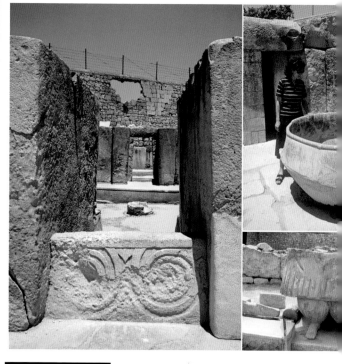

TIP

● Tarxien and the Hypogeum
(▷ 50–51) are part of a
connected complex. Tarxien
relates to the ceremonies of
life while the Hypogeum to
the ceremonies of death and
the afterlife. You should try
to see both.

**The most extensive of Malta's temple
complexes, Tarxien is also the most
instantly appreciable of the megalithic
sites. Here you can see all the
architectural and decorative techniques
that mark the Temple Builders' style.**

The site Discovered in 1913 by local farmers
working the land, the site was excavated into
the 1920s. Tarxien has four trefoil temple structures, and was in use throughout the Temple
Building era but much of the site dates from
late in the timeline.

The temples The most highly decorated of the
temples shows a distinct development in art
from Ħaġar Qim (▷ 49) and Ġgantija on Gozo
(▷ 98–99), with complex animal reliefs and

spiral patterns. The bottom half of a monumental voluptuous skirted fertility goddess/priestess statue is matched by smaller found statues on display in the National Museum of Archaeology (▷ 32). The easternmost temple is the earliest, dating from c. 3600BC, around the same time as Ħaġar Qim, but it is not in good condition and is separated from the other three. The central temple of Tarxien is the largest on Malta, with six apses leading from a short central nave. The south temple is the youngest, c. 2800BC, and is the most highly decorated. The relief carving of two bulls and a sow on the wall between the south and central temples is the finest megalithic art found to date on Malta and suggests a community well versed in animal husbandry. It also suggests fertility rights and animal sacrifice, as the libation altars here seem to confirm.

THE BASICS

www.heritagemalta.org
➕ H7
✉ Neolithic Temples Street, Tarxien
☎ 21695578
🕐 Daily 9–5
🚌 8, 11, 27, 29, 30 from Valletta
♿ Few
💰 Moderate

The Three Cities

HIGHLIGHTS

- The *vedette*'s superb views
- Vittoriosa waterfront
- The Malta at War Museum
- The Inquisitor's Palace
- The Maritime Museum

TIPS

- In the Collachio there are eight *auberges*, some from the Norman era.
- Look for Cottonera Lines: 5km (3 miles) of fortifications.
- Vintage Bus Sightseeing offers tours (tel 21694967; www.supremecoaches.com).

Birgu was the Knights' first home on Malta, then they expanded to Il'Isla and Bormla. The Three Cities had some of the biggest dockyards in the Mediterranean. Today, Vittoriosa (Birgu) has plenty to see; views of Valletta are breathtaking.

Vittoriosa/Birgu Founded by the Normans in the 11th century, Birgu was the Knights' headquarters before they built Valletta. After the victory of the Great Siege they renamed the town Vittoriosa. Today it's an architectural treasure-trove. The heart of the town, the Collachio, was once the enclave of the Order and has atmospheric alleyways with medieval *auberges* and *palazzos*. Here you will also find the Inquisitor's Palace (▷ 61). Vittoriosa's Dockyard Creek was an important naval base

Clockwise from far left: Wrought-iron balconies in Victory Square, Vittoriosa; narrow street in Vittoriosa; church of the Immaculate Conception, Cospicua; traditional dghajsas, Senglea; ear and eye carvings on the vedette, Senglea

from the 16th to the 20th century, so visit the Malta Maritime Museum (▷ 62). Fortifications abound: at the Grand Harbour end is Fort St. Angelo (▷ 61) and the Malta at War Museum (▷ 62) is in the landward city gate.

Senglea/Il'Isla Named Senglea after Grand Master Claude de la Sengle, the town has a more workaday image than Birgu. The *vedette* (lookout point) at Senglea Point offers a magnificent view across Grand Harbour (▷ 28–29). Look for the carved eyes and ears on its flanks; symbols of vigilance.

Cospicua/Bormla Bormla, at the head of Dockyard Creek, was named Cospicua (meaning noteworthy) after the Great Siege. The Knights built their original shipyard here.

THE BASICS

✚ H6
✉ 4km (2.5 miles) south of Valletta
🍴 Cafés and restaurants
🚌 1, 4, 6 from Valletta, 627 from Buġibba, 881 (night service) from Paceville; 3 to Senglea from Valletta
❓ An oar-powered water-taxi, or *dghajsa,* operates to Vittoriosa from Valletta. Book your crossing (tel 21806921; www. maltesewatertaxis.com)

More to See

BUSKETT GARDENS
Planned by Grand Master Lascaris during the 17th century as a hunting and recreation ground, Buskett Gardens is a good location to escape the heat of summer. In its Mediterranean woodlands, citrus orchards and olive groves with cooling springs, you can enjoy a stroll and a picnic.
🔁 D7 ✉ 4km (2.5 miles) south of Rabat ⏱ Open access 🍴 Restaurant open May–Oct 🚌 81 from Valletta/Rabat ♿ Few 🗓 Free

CLAPHAM JUNCTION
Misraħ Għar il-Kbir is a collection of grooves dating from c.2000BC, worn deep into the limestone substrate. It was given the name Clapham Junction by the British, because the grooves resembled the many lines at the busy UK rail interchange of the same name. There is debate about how the grooves were formed, though the most popular theory is that they were eroded by sleds used to transport goods. There are many examples across Malta and Gozo—signposted 'cart ruts' on maps and road signs—but Clapham Junction is the most impressive.
🔁 D7 ✉ 0.5km (0.3miles) south of Buskett Gardens ⏱ Open access 🚌 81 from Valletta/Rabat ♿ None 🗓 Free

DINGLI CLIFFS
The sheer limestone cliffs on Malta's west coast offer some of the finest vistas on the island. Whatever time of year, this is a lovely place to enjoy a stroll. You are around 200m (650ft) above sea level but the terrain is almost flat. Standing sentinel is the small chapel of St. Magdalena, built in 1646.
🔁 C7 ✉ 0.5km (0.3 miles) from Dingli village 🍴 Bobbyland restaurant (€€) 🚌 81 from Valletta/Rabat ♿ None 🗓 Free

FORT RINELLA
www.wirtartna.org
In the late 19th century, Grand Harbour was vulnerable to a new class of Italian warship, so the

Grooved limestone of Clapham Junction resembles railway tracks

Royal Navy commissioned two 100-tonne guns: one for each flank of the harbour mouth. Each gun required a fort to protect it, though Fort Rinella is the only one remaining. It is a low-lying fortification with concrete underground chambers and dense earthworks to protect from seaward bombardment. The Armstrong 100-tonne gun here is the largest muzzle-loading cannon ever built. Its 1-tonne shell could pierce 53cm (21 inches) of armour and had a maximum effective range of 6.4km (4 miles). However, the gun was declared obsolete in 1906, overtaken by technological advances. At 2.30pm, costumed staff conduct a guided tour of the fort, with drill and gunfire practice.

🞡 J6 ✉ St. Rocco Road, Kalkara
☎ 21809713 🕘 Tue–Sun 10–5; guided tours on the hour 🍽 Café 🚌 627 from Buġibba (via Sliema). Free transport to and from the Saluting Battery in Valletta (▷ 39) and the Malta at War Museum (▷ 62)
🚹 Few 💰 Expensive; combined tickets to Wirt Artna attractions: expensive

GĦAR DALAM
www.heritagemalta.org
The earliest evidence of human activity on Malta was found here, in what in Maltese means 'Cave of Darkness'. The cave was also the route of a river in prehistoric times and the fossils of thousands of animals were found in the cave floor, making it one of the most complete strata of Pleistocene deposits in Europe. The lowermost deposits (500,000 years old) contain fossil remains of dwarf elephants and hippo but the cave first saw human activity c.6000–5000bc. It was in use until the Temple Building period began. It is possible to tour part of the cave, and the small museum on site is fascinating. It is packed with fossils. The most important human artefacts are now on display at the National Museum of Archaeology in Valletta (▷ 32).

🞡 J8 ✉ Zeytun Road, Birżebbuġa
☎ 21657419 🕘 Daily 9–5 🚌 11, 12 from Valletta/Birżebbuġa 🚹 None
💰 Moderate

Għar Dalam bears much evidence of early animal life

MARSAXLOKK

Arguably the island's prettiest waterfront vista, Marsaxlokk (pronounced Marsa-shlok) harbour is home to Malta's inshore fishing fleet of multi-hued wooden *luzzu*. There's a daily market, Sunday morning fish market and a good choice of restaurants offering a tasty fish lunch.

🞠 J8 ✉ 10km (6 miles) southeast of Valletta 🚌 27, 29, 30 from Valletta, 627 from Buġibba

QRENDI

South of the village of Qrendi (pronounced Rendi) is Il-Maqluba, a sinkhole 100m (330ft) in diameter and 50m (165ft) deep, created by the collapse of the underlying limestone, thought to have happened during a storm in 1343. Maltese legend tells that the sinkhole was created by God to punish evildoers. The chapel of St. Catherine Tat-Torba (1625) has a plain facade.

🞠 F8 🕐 Il-Maqluba: open access 🍴 Café in Qrendi village 🚌 35 from Valletta ♿ None 🛈 Il-Maqluba: free

SIĠĠIEWI

In one of 10 original parishes of Malta, the highly ornate baroque church of St. Nicholas of Bari befits the important town of Siġġiewi (pronounced Sidgiwi). Inaugurated in 1729 to a design by Lorenzo Gafà, it was enlarged in the 1860s. The titular painting of St. Nicholas is by Mattia Preti. Limestone Heritage (www.limestoneheritage.com), just south of the town bypass, tells the story of one of Malta's most important raw materials, its characteristic limestone rock. This rock built Valletta and Mdina, and the hundreds of churches that dot the landscape. Limestone Heritage is set in a disused limestone quarry, worked until the late 20th century, and is an excellent museum showing the techniques of how the stone was cut and transported. A workshop showcases artisans working the stone, and there is a traditional Maltese farmhouse, or *razzett*. Around 5km (3 miles) south of the town, the old Inquisitor's Summer

Traditional luzzu fishing boats in Marsaxlokk harbour

Palace, built in 1625, is now a summer residence of the Maltese Prime Minister and off-limits to the public.
🔒 E7 ✉ 8km (5 miles) southwest of Valletta 🍴 Café in town, and at Limestone Heritage (▷ 66) 🚌 89, 94 from Valletta

THE THREE CITIES: FORT ST. ANGELO

The Knights made Castello a Mare, the Aragonese fort on the Birgu headland, their headquarters when they arrived in Malta in 1530, renaming it Fort St. Angelo. The walls withstood the Great Siege against the Turks in 1565, but soon afterwards the Knights moved to Valletta. During British rule the fort was Royal Navy property and in World War II the armaments were an important protection for the naval dockyards. The fort now stands neglected, but parts have been leased back to the Knights of St. John and their flag can be seen flying over the complex.
🔒 H6 ✉ Birgu headland 🕐 Not open to the public 🚌 To Vittoriosa: 1, 4, 6 from

Valletta, 627 from Buġibba, 881 (night service) from Paceville

THE THREE CITIES: INQUISITOR'S PALACE

www.heritagemalta.org

Pope Paul III (1534–49) instigated the Roman Inquisition and the Catholic Church sent the first Inquisitor to Malta in 1574. The Knights offered this existing medieval courthouse (1530) as a seat and the Inquisition remained here until 1798. Subsequent Inquisitors expanded and upgraded it through the centuries, including the gardens (1634), the prison (1639), the private apartments (1694), and the main portal and staircase (1731). The Inquisition departed when the French arrived and during British rule the palace was used as a military hospital and officers' mess.
🔒 H6 ✉ Main Gate Street, Vittoriosa
☎ 21827006 🕐 Daily 9–5 🚌 To Vittoriosa: 1, 4, 6 from Valletta, 627 from Buġibba, 881 (night service) from Paceville ♿ Few
💰 Moderate

Marble statue of St. Nicholas, near the church dedicated to him in Siġġiewi

Fort St. Angelo, from Valletta fortifications

THE THREE CITIES: THE MALTA AT WAR MUSEUM

www.wirtartna.org

These old military barracks in the Main Gate offer one of the most poignant reminders of Malta's tribulations during World War II. Beneath ground is the only remaining public air-raid shelter in the south of Malta. Cut by the people themselves in the first days of the war, it is an extensive maze of corridors and rooms where thousands of Maltese lived full time during the bombardment of 1942–43. The guided tours add a wealth of personal detail. Watch *Malta G. C.*, a film commissioned by the British government in the wake of the siege, which shows the devastation.

➕ H6 ✉ Main Gate, Vittoriosa
☎ 21896617 🕐 Tue–Sun 10–5 🚌 To Vittoriosa: 1, 4, 6 from Valletta, 627 from Buġibba, 881 (night service) from Paceville. Free transport links the museum with the Saluting Battery (▷ 39) and Fort Rinella (▷ 58–59) ♿ Few 💷 Moderate; multi-site ticket: expensive

THE THREE CITIES: MALTA MARITIME MUSEUM

www.heritagemalta.org

The Old Naval Bakery building is packed with maritime memorabilia spanning the age of the Knights through to the end of British rule. It's a fascinating mixture of technical equipment, personal items and paintings, including a huge canvas of the Santa Maria, the *carrack* that brought the Knights to Malta.

➕ H6 ✉ Vittoriosa waterfront ☎ 21660052
🕐 Daily 9–5 🍴 Restaurants on the waterfront 🚌 To Vittoriosa: 1, 4, 6 from Valletta, 627 from Buġibba, 881 (night service) from Paceville ♿ Few 💷 Moderate

THE THREE CITIES: ST. JOSEPH'S ORATORY

This chapel was built in 1832, abutting St. Lawrence Collegiate Church. Today, it's a small museum housing an eclectic collection linked to the Knights and the Inquisition, including the hat and sword worn by Grand Master La Valette, gifted in thanks for the relief of Vittoriosa.

The Malta Maritime Museum on Vittoriosa waterfront

🔶 H6 ✉ Vittoriosa Square ⊙ Daily
9.30–12 🍽 Restaurants nearby 🚌 To
Vittoriosa: 1 4, 6 from Valletta, 627 from
Buġibba, 881 (night service) from Paceville
♿ None 👆 Free

VERDALA PALACE

Built in 1586 among lush forests
as a summer palace, Verdala Palace
was embellished by several Grand
Masters. Later it became a prison
and a silk factory, before being
restored in the 1850s by the then
Governor, Sir William Reid. It is
now the summer residence of the
Maltese President.

🔶 D7 ✉ 3km (2 miles) southeast of Rabat
⊙ Not open to the public 🚌 80, 81, 84
from Valletta, 65 from Sliema

ŻABBAR

During the Great Siege, Ottoman
forces set their main encampment
here, just beyond the landward fortifications that protected the Three
Cities (▷ 56–57). The town was
granted city status by Ferdinand de
Hompesch, the last Grand Master.

Maltese opposition to French rule
was galvanized here, and the town
suffered massive damage from
French bombardment. Tommaso
Dingli's Church of Our Lady of
Graces (1640) has been given
an ornate baroque makeover. The
Sanctuary Museum (Sun 9–12)
displays votive paintings.

🔶 J6 ✉ 7km (4 miles) south of Valletta
🚌 18, 21 from Valletta, 22 from Cospicua, 19
from Marsaskala

ŻURRIEQ

One of the 10 original medieval
parishes on Malta, Żurrieq is now
a quiet market town. The parish
church, dedicated to St. Catherine
of Alexandria, is not as ornate as
others on the island but benefits
from Mattia Preti original paintings.
Just outside the town, the diminutive chapel of Ħal-Millieri Church of
the Annunciation (first Sun of the
month 9–12) dates from around
1480 and has Byzantine frescoes.

🔶 G8 ✉ 9.5km (5.5 miles) south of Valletta
🚌 32, 34 from Valletta

Sun lights the steps of Verdala Palace

The massive Żabbar Gate

Malta's Far Southwest

Explore the range of natural and man-made attractions in Malta's southwestern corner, only a few miles from Valletta.

DISTANCE: 29km (18 miles) **ALLOW:** 6–8 hours with stops

START

RABAT
✚ D6

① Leave the town by heading west on route 16, signposted Dingli. Drive through Dingli village to Dingli Cliffs (▷ 58). Take time to wander along the cliff tops enjoying the breezes.

② Return to Dingli village and turn right, signposted Buskett. Buskett Gardens (▷ 58) have extensive woodlands and are a magnet for local families in summer months.

③ Continue along the road as it swings back to the coast. In the countryside to the left is the maze of cart ruts known as Clapham Junction (▷ 58).

④ Keep travelling along this road as it turns left along the coast for a while, then inland again on a winding route to Siġġiewi (▷ 60).

END

RABAT

⑧ After 1.25km (0.75 miles), turn right to San Blas/Mdina/Rabat and the road leads 3.75km (2.3 miles) across the island to Rabat/Mdina.

⑦ From the Blue Grotto, return to Siġġiewi and turn left at the main roundabout previously visited.

⑥ After visiting the temples, return to the main road and turn right. The road leads on down to the Blue Grotto (▷ 48). The viewpoint is a good spot for photos.

⑤ Leave Siġġiewi, taking the route south in the direction of Ħaġar Qim and the Blue Grotto. After 2.5km (1.5 miles), the road sweeps left along a ridge and it is another 2.5km (1.5 miles) until the turning to Ħaġar Qim (▷ 49) appears on the right.

THE SOUTH

DRIVE

Shopping

SHOPPING

THE SOUTH

FORT RINELLA

There's a range of books here relating to military history in Malta. Though the fort dates from the Victorian era, the books cover the arrival of the Knights, through French rule, on to World War II and to the British withdrawal in the latter part of the 20th century.
➕ J6 ✉ St. Rocco Road, Kalkara ☎ 21809713 🕐 Tue–Sun 10–5 🚌 627 from Buġibba (via Sliema). Free transport to and from the Saluting Battery in Valletta (▷ 39) and the Malta at War Museum (▷ 62)

LIMESTONE HERITAGE

www.limestoneheritage.com
Voted best attraction retail space in Malta in 2008 and 2009, Limestone Heritage sells an excellent range of items carved by the artisans who work at the site, so you won't find these anywhere else on the island. They also stock a good range of Maltese delicacies including honey and a range of souvenirs.
➕ F7 ✉ Triq Mons. M. Azzopardi, Siġġiewi ☎ 21464931 🕐 Mon–Fri 9–3, Sat 9–12, Sun 8.30–11.30 🚌 None direct; 89, 94 from Valletta

MARSAXLOKK DAILY MARKET

The vendors set up around the harbour front and sell a range of souvenirs and Maltese edible treats, but the market is famed for its textiles, ranging from tea towels to table cloths. Much of what is on sale is mass-produced and imported but it is still a good choice.
➕ J8 ✉ Xatt is-Sajjieda (harbour front), Marsaxlokk 🕐 Daily 9–4 🚌 27, 29, 30 from Valletta, 627 from Buġibba

MARSAXLOKK FISH MARKET

Every Sunday morning the fishing fleet lands its catch and sells it along the harbour front. Although you may not have facilities to cook, this is a fun experience.
➕ J8 ✉ Xatt is-Sajjieda (harbour front), Marsaxlokk 🕐 Sun 9–12 🚌 27, 29, 30 from Valletta, 627 from Buġibba

MARSOVIN

www.marsovin.com
A full range of Marsovin wines are on sale at their

GRAPE VINE

International wines are available but you should really try a few of the Maltese and Gozitan wines. Many of the labels are blends incorporating the major grape varieties. However, native grapes are still useful, being adapted to the climate and soil conditions. Look for the names *ghirgentina*, for a fresh, light crisp white, and *gellewza*, a light and fruity red.

---

shop, including the cellar-aged vintages dating back to 1998. You can stock up after the cellar tour and tasting. There are other Marsovin products on sale, including glasses. Wines are also available at the airport, making them duty free (therefore cheaper) for all travellers heading out of Europe.
➕ G6 ✉ The Winery, Wills Street, Marsa ☎ 21824918 🕐 Mon–Fri 9–5 🚌 None

PLAYMOBIL FUNPARK

www.playmobilmalta.com
Children love Playmobil figures and accessories, and there's an excellent variety on sale at the Playmobil Funpark shop. The Knights product range is a popular purchase from Malta.
➕ H9 ✉ HF80, Industrial Estate, Ħal Far ☎ 22242445 🕐 Oct–Jun daily 10–6; Jul–Sep Mon–Sat 10–6, Sun 10–1 🚌 13 from Valletta

STREETCRAFT

www.streetcraft.com
Goran Carevic and his wife Lourdes settled on Malta from Croatia and have built a solid reputation for their hand-crafted jewellery in the 12 years since they arrived. Their strong and vibrant pieces complement summer fashions, and make use of semi-precious stones, glass and crystal.
➕ J6 ✉ 54 Triq il-Kbira, Żabbar ☎ 21894771 🕐 Mon–Fri 9–5 🚌 None

Entertainment and Activities

CASINO DI VENEZIA

www.casinodivenezia.com.mt
Offering a range of games from roulette to Black Jack, this casino set in an Italianate *palazzo* on the Vittoriosa waterfront is the place to come to enjoy a flutter.

⊞ f5 ⊠ Vittoriosa waterfront ☎ 23979130 🕐 Gaming tables: Mon–Thu 2pm–2am, Fri–Sun 2pm–4am; slot machines: Mon–Fri 2pm–2am, Sat 2pm–4am, Sun noon–4am 🚌 To Vittoriosa: 1, 4, 6 from Valletta, 627 from Buġibba, 881 (night service) from Paceville

CHAPTER'S THE CLUB

This open-air venue is one of the liveliest places on Malta for drinking and dancing in the summer months. It hosts guest DJs and promotes occasional live music performances.

⊞ K7 ⊠ Triq Il-Gardiel, Marsaskala 🕐 Fri–Sun 10pm–3am 🚌 18, 19, 20, 21, 22 from Valletta

THE KNIGHTS SPECTACULAR 1565

www.malta1565.com
This thrilling live family dinner show brings the representatives of the Knights of St. John and the Ottoman armies face to face once more, with the crack of gunpowder and some phenomenal displays of horsemanship, along with a song and dance accompaniment. There is transport available to the venue

organized from various hotels around Malta.

⊞ F7 ⊠ The Arena, Montekristo Estates, Ħal Farruġ, Siġġiewi ☎ Administration: 21228065; ticketline: 99991565 🕐 Thu evenings 🚌 None

MALTA FOLKLORE NIGHTS

Enjoy dancers and musicians in traditional costume performing *festa*, fishermen's, farmer's and wedding dances, while tucking into a buffet of Maltese and Gozitan dishes. It is all set in the open courtyard of Limestone Heritage.

⊞ F7 ⊠ Mons. M. Azzopardi, Siġġiewi ☎ 21464931 🕐 May–Sep Tue and Thu 🚌 None direct; 89, 94 from Valletta

PLAYMOBIL FUNPARK

www.playmobilmalta.com
This small fun-park is stocked with slides and giant Playmobil models for children to climb on. It's a great place for

FILIGREE

Tradition says that it was the Phoenicians who introduced filigree to Malta. Over the centuries the craft has been passed down, often through generations of the same family. Filigree became a popular gift and souvenir through medieval times into the modern era; perhaps because it's light and easy to transport.

youngsters to play for an hour or two.

⊞ H9 ⊠ HF80, Industrial Estate, Ħal Far ☎ 22242445 🕐 Oct–Jun daily 10–6; Jul–Sep Mon–Sat 10–6, Sun 10–1 🚌 13 from Valletta

SALIBA'S GOLD AND SILVERSMITH

www.salibafiligree.com
Saliba's is an important supplier of filigree jewellery to the trade, but if you want to learn how to make your own souvenirs, they also run filigree courses. These are short taster sessions to craftsmen standard.

⊞ K7 ⊠ 19 Triq il-Kavetti, Marsaskala ☎ 26137508 🕐 Courses run to demand 🚌 None direct; 18, 19, 20, 21, 22 from Valletta

STRAIT STREET THE MUSICAL

From the time of the Knights until the closing of the British bases, Strait Street in Valletta (also known as The Gut) was Malta's notorious red-light district. *Strait Street the Musical*, an evening show, takes an entertaining and light-hearted look at Maltese history from a rather cheeky and off-the-wall perspective. A snack platter is served during the performance. Parental guidance suggested for younger children.

⊞ f5 ⊠ The Arena, Montekristo Estates, Ħal Farruġ, Siġġiewi ☎ Administration: 21228065; Ticketline 99991565 🕐 Tue evenings 🚌 None

Restaurants

BLUE CREEK BAR & RESTAURANT (€€–€€€)

www.bluecreekmalta.com
The sea views down the cliffs into Għar Lapsi cove from this restaurant are spectacular. The à la carte menu offers some tasty Mediterranean dishes, and they also serve a selection of sandwiches and salads.

➕ E8 ✉ Għar Lapsi ☎ 21462800 🕒 Mon, Wed, Fri–Sun lunch and dinner, Thu lunch 🚌 94 from Valletta

CAFÉ DE PARIS (€)

On the harbour front this cheap and cheerful eatery offers an excellent set lunch of rabbit or local fish, along with a carafe of Maltese wine. It's a no-frills set-up with tables by the water.

➕ J8 ✉ Xatt is-Sajjieda, Marsaxlokk ☎ 21650652 🕒 Daily lunch and dinner 🚌 27, 29, 30 from Valletta, 627 from Buġibba

CONCEPT CAFÉ (€)

This 19th-century mansion has been converted into a complex comprising several eateries. Concept Café is a bright contemporary space on the ground floor. You can enjoy a plate of pasta, or a sandwich or wrap, and there are daily specials for lunch. Alternatively, simply stop for a coffee and a delicious pastry.

➕ J8 ✉ Southport Villa and Gardens, Xatt is-Sajjieda, Marsaxlokk ☎ 27012600 🕒 Daily 9am–11pm 🚌 27, 29, 30 from Valletta, 627 from Buġibba

HUNTER'S TOWER RESTAURANT AND PIZZERIA (€€)

In business for more than 30 years, Hunter's Tower is a large modern restaurant with an airy garden at the rear. It serves a good range of fish, in addition to pasta, pizza and a few Maltese dishes.

➕ J8 ✉ Wilga Street, Marsaxlokk ☎ 21651792 🕒 May–Sep daily lunch and dinner; Oct–Apr Tue–Thu

YOUR FISHY LEXICON

Maltese / English	
accola / amberjack	
barbun Imperjali / turbot	
cerna or dott / grouper	
incova / anchovy	
klamer / squid	
lampuka / dolphinfish	
lingwata / sole	
marlozz / hake	
mulett / mullet	
palamit / skipjack tuna	
pixxipad / swordfish	
san pietro / john dory	
sardina kahla / pilchard	
sargu / sea bream	
sawrella / mackerel	

lunch, Fri–Sun lunch and dinner 🚌 27, 29, 30 from Valletta, 627 from Buġibba

IR-RIZZU (€€)

www.ir-rizzu.com
This is one of the best fish restaurants on the island, serving dishes made from the fresh catch of the day.

➕ J8 ✉ Xatt is-Sajjieda, Marsaxlokk ☎ 21651569 🕒 Daily lunch and dinner 🚌 27, 29, 30 from Valletta, 627 from Buġibba

RIVIERA DELLA MARINA (€€–€€€)

www.tritonmalta.com
The vaulted dining rooms set in the old captain-ary are surprisingly cosy, but there's also a terrace overlooking the Vittoriosa Marina. The menu concentrates on fresh seafood and pasta.

➕ f5 ✉ Vittoriosa waterfront ☎ 21242007 🕒 Daily lunch and dinner 🚌 To Vittoriosa: 1, 4, 6 from Valletta, 627 from Buġibba, 881 (night service) from Paceville

TAL-FAMILJA (€–€€)

www.talfamiljarestaurant.com
This family-owned restaurant has an excellent reputation with the locals. The menu features a range of both Maltese and Mediterranean dishes and wines.

➕ K7 ✉ Triq il-Gardiel, Marsaskala ☎ 21632361 🕒 Tue–Sun lunch and dinner 🚌 18, 19, 20, 21, 22 from Valletta

The Centre and the North

In the centre and the north are some of Malta's best historical attractions at Mdina and Rabat, its liveliest resorts at chic Sliema/St. Julian's and cheerful St. Paul's Bay, and acres of wild countryside.

Sights	72–85
Drive	86
Walk	87
Shopping	88
Entertainment and Activities	89
Restaurants	90

Top 25

TOP
25

Mdina ▷ 72
Mdina: St. Paul's Cathedral ▷ 74
Mosta Rotunda ▷ 75
Naxxar: Palazzo Parisio ▷ 76
Rabat: St. Paul's & St. Agatha's Catacombs ▷ 77
Sliema ▷ 78

Licata, Pozzallo

0   3 km

0   2 miles

Qawra Point
(Il-Ponta tal-Qawra)
Ghallis Point
(Il-Ponta ta' l-Ghallis)
Ghallis Rocks
(Gebel ta' l-Ghallis)

Qrejten Point
(Ponta tal-Qrejten)

Il-Hotba
I-Bajda

Il-Maghtab

San Pietru   Victoria Lines   Madliena   Pembroke

Gharghur   Il-Mielah   Swieqi   St George's Bay
                   Ta' Gokondu   (Il-Bajja ta' San Gorg)
Palazzo   Paceville
Parisio   Ix-Xwieki   Ta' l-Ghoqod   Balluta
Naxxar   Is Simblija   Bay
Rosta   St Julian's   Sliema Point
Rotunda   San Gwann   Ta' Giorni   Sliema
                            Kappara   Gzira
          Iklin   Il-Qasbija   San Gwann   Sliema Creek   Dragut Point
                              tal-Gharghar   (Il-Ponta Dragut)
Hal-Mirakli   Lija   Manoel
                                          Island
          Balzan   Birkirkara   Msida   Ta' Xbiex
Attard   Fleur de Lys
Tisrah   Santa Venera   Pieta
Kola   Ta' Qassati   Gwardamanga
              Tad-Dwieli   Tas-Samra   Hamrun
          Il-Hammieri   Il-Bajjada
              Qormi
Hal-   Ta' l-Infatti   L-Armier   L-Istabar
Luxi   Zebbug   Ghar-Ram
          Hal-Dwien

F   G   H

Mdina

HIGHLIGHTS

- Palazzo Falson
- St. Paul's Cathedral
- Views from Bastion Square
- The maze of alleys flanked by medieval stone mansions

TIPS

- A little train from Mdina tours Rabat (▷ 82). For details visit www.melitatrains.com or tel 79212142.
- Take the Discover Mdina audiotour (▷ 73).
- Watch out for horse-drawn carriages in narrow alleys.

Capital of Malta before the arrival of the Knights, Mdina is a magnificent fortified hilltop enclave, whose narrow alleyways are redolent of the medieval past. Fine views can be had from the walls.

History Settled since Phoenician times (c.700BC), the town expanded under the Romans as Melita, from the Greek for honey; also the derivation of the word Malta. The Arabs renamed the town Mdina and fortified part of it, separating it from neighbouring Rabat (named from the Arabic for suburb). The Normans made Mdina their capital, and seat of the Catholic Bishop of Malta. When Malta was handed over to the Knights, they felt the city was too remote from the coast and settled at Birgu (▷ 56). Mdina lost its political influence

Clockwise from far left: The gate to Palazzo Vilhena; statue of the Madonna and Child on a wall; aerial view of the fortified town; view from the bastion walls; quiet street in the town

but remained the religious centre of the island; a role it still holds. Badly damaged by an earthquake in 1693, the city was rebuilt in baroque style. The fine gateway dates from this era. Many of the *palazzos* and mansions belong to religious orders. Today it's home to fewer than 300 people and is known as 'The Silent City'.

Major attractions In Mdina you can enjoy the architecture as much as the attractions. The baroque Cathedral of St. Paul (▷ 74) dominates the skyline. Norman Palazzo Falson (▷ 81) and Palazzo Santa Sophia (*c.*1233) give a good feel of how mansions would have looked before the earthquake, while Palazzo Vilhena (erected *c.*1720) houses Malta's Natural History Museum. Bastion Square has excellent long-range views.

THE BASICS

✠ D6

✉ 11km (6.5 miles) south-west of Valletta

🍽 Cafés and restaurants

🚌 80, 81 from Valletta, 65 from Sliema, 86 from Buġibba

❓ Discover Mdina audiotour (moderate) has information to accompany your visit. This can be rented at Palazzo Vilhena, just beyond the main gate as you enter the city

Mdina: St. Paul's Cathedral

Looking into the dome (left); the interior (middle); the exterior (right)

THE BASICS

➕ D6
✉ St. Paul's Square, Mdina
☎ 21454136
🕐 Mon–Sat 9–5
🍴 Cafés and restaurants nearby
🚌 None direct; to Mdina: 80, 81 from Valletta, 65 from Sliema, 86 from Buġibba
♿ Few
🖐 Church and museum: inexpensive

DID YOU KNOW?

● Roman Governor Publius converted to Christianity after Paul's stay on Malta. As the Christian community developed, he was appointed the first Bishop and was martyred for his faith in AD125.

TIP

● The floor is a maze of tombstones, but unlike the Co-Cathedral (▷ 35), these are tombs of the clergy and Maltese nobility, not Knights.

St. Paul's Cathedral shares the limelight with St. John's Co-Cathedral in Valletta in terms of status, but they have different atmospheres. Although baroque in style, this is the restrained mode of the Vatican.

History of the site The cathedral stands on the traditional site of the mansion of the Roman Governor Publius, location of his conversion to Christianity by St. Paul in AD60. After Arab rule, the Normans built a place of worship befitting the seat of the Catholic Bishop of Malta in the late 11th century. This Norman church was badly damaged in the earthquake of 1693 and it was decided to rebuild it in much grander and luxurious style. This new design, by Lorenzo Gafà, incorporated an old city block, including an open square in front of the building. The new cathedral was consecrated in 1703.

Art and architecture This is considered Gafà's *tour de force*, balancing the facade towers and dome to achieve pleasing proportions. The interior is typical of the ornate baroque style, yet features elements salvaged from the Norman church. These include works by Mattia Preti (1613–99); the best is a monumental canvas depicting the conversion of St. Paul.

The museum Housed in the old seminary is one of the richest collections of religious art and treasures in Europe. There are also Punic and Roman finds from old Melita, and woodcarvings by Albrecht Dürer (1471–1528).

Mosta Rotunda

Front elevation of the church (left); the stunning interior (right)

Mosta's Church of the Assumption—known as Mosta Rotunda or Mosta Dome—harks back to the architectural style of the Classical era, but its more recent history adds frisson to your visit.

Distinctive design By the early 1800s the population of Mosta had outgrown its small chapel and put out tenders for a new building. The circular design by George Grognet de Vasse was chosen by parish priest Fr. Don Felice Calleja because it reminded him of the Pantheon in Rome, where he had experienced his first high mass. Work started in 1833, the build was completed in 1860 and the church was dedicated in 1871.

Classical proportions A neoclassical facade with the statues of six saints incorporates the main portal. Once inside, the expansive proportions of the interior and its unsupported dome—the fourth largest in Europe—is immediately apparent. Six niches radiate from the central space, each with a small chapel.

Sacristy Two silver altar facades are the religious highlights of the sacristy. One depicts the Battle of Lepanto in 1571, when the Knights and other Catholic forces won a decisive naval victory over the Ottoman Empire. On 9 April 1942, a bomb pierced the dome and rolled down the aisle. It did not explode and there were only minor injuries to the congregation of 300. A copy of the shell is displayed.

THE BASICS

🔲 E5
📧 Church Street, Mosta
☎ 21418368
🕐 Daily 9–11.45, 3–5
🍴 Cafés and restaurants nearby
🚌 47, 49 (night service), 52, 58, 59, 159 from Valletta, 427 from Buġibba
♿ Few
💷 Free

HIGHLIGHTS

● The sheer scale of the unsupported dome
● The story of the unexploded bomb

TIPS

● Mosta celebrates during Holy Week at Easter and also on the feast of the Assumption (15 August), when the church is lit with thousands of bulbs and processions fill the streets.
● Look for damage in the dome roof above the sacristy door, caused by the bomb.

Naxxar: Palazzo Parisio

TOP 25

The garden and palazzo (left); the ornate baroque ballroom (right)

The interior of Palazzo Parisio is a dazzling showcase of the personal taste of 'mover and shaker', Marquis Giuseppe Scicluna. This is how the Maltese upper classes lived in the 19th century.

Family history Built in 1733 by Grand Master Manoel de Vilhena, the palace became a country retreat for the noble Parisio family. In the mid-19th century, Scicluna—whose family introduced banking to Malta—restored the whole estate. His son, Giovanni, went on to found the first brewery on Malta.

The house Giuseppe created a home to suit the needs of a rich businessman and socialite. These included a study and an enormous billiard room. The Lombarda Room, decorated in the fashionable Lombardy style, has art works by Mattia Preti, while a large Filippo Venuti canvas in the Pompeian Dining Room depicts a rural scene from Naxxar. The ballroom is 'Versailles in miniature', blanketed in gilded stucco, mirrors and crystal. The frescoes are allegories depicting art, astronomy, theatre and literature. The Grand Staircase to the *piano nobile* is an impressive creation of Carrara marble. The handrail is carved from one solid piece.

The garden The formal baroque-style gardens comprise four lawns with boxed hedges and terraces immediately beyond the French windows of the Great Hall, and a second garden focusing on a large Italianate fountain.

TOP 25

Rabat: St. Paul's & St. Agatha's Catacombs

The arched catacombs in which St. Paul sheltered (left); fresco of St. Agatha and St. Paul (right)

THE CENTRE AND THE NORTH

★ TOP 25

This extensive Roman burial complex is one of the finest of its kind in the world. The chambers give us a unique perspective on the transition from pagan to monotheistic faith on Malta.

St. Paul's Catacombs These catacombs are extensive. At the foot of the entrance steps are two large chambers supported by Doric columns. The carved platforms with sloping sides and tables are thought to have been used for ceremonial meals shared by the living relatives on the anniversary of the demise of the deceased. A series of passages leads from a central hall to vaulted chambers with canopied graves for adult bodies and niches or loculi for babies and infants, all hand-dug out of the limestone. The catacombs were used by the early Christian community and are the oldest evidence of organized Christianity on the island. Part of the complex was also reused after the Arabs left Malta, when one of the chambers was transformed into a Christian shrine, the walls decorated with murals in Byzantine style.

St. Agatha's Catacombs Legend tells us that this natural cave was where St. Agatha stayed while on the run from Roman persecution (AD249–251), before returning to Sicily where she was promptly tortured and imprisoned, dying a martyr in 251. She is one of Malta's patron saints. The cave was expanded into an underground complex with several single chamber chapels and a small church built above.

THE BASICS

www.heritagemalta.org
✚ D6
✉ St. Agatha Street, Rabat
☎ 21454562
🕐 Daily 9–5
🍴 Cafés and restaurants nearby
🚌 80, 81 from Valletta, 65 from Sliema, 86 from Buġibba
♿ Few
💷 Moderate

HIGHLIGHTS

● Frescoes in the chapels at St. Agatha's Catacombs
● The grand chambers of St. Paul's Catacombs

TIP

● The vibrant Christian Byzantine frescoes here, depicting St. Agatha and other saints, are the best of their style on Malta.

Sliema

Seafront promenade (left); a bus in the resort (middle); Sliema Creek (right)

THE BASICS

➕ H5

✉ 7km (4 miles) west of Valletta

🚌 62 (night service), 64, 66, 67, 68, 662, 667, 671 from Valletta, 65 from Mdina/Rabat, 645, 652 from Ċirkewwa, 627 from Three Cities/Marsaxlokk, 49 (night service) from Mosta

⛴ Ferry to Valletta

HIGHLIGHTS

● Shopping
● Nightlife
● Restaurants and bars
● Hotels

TIP

● Night bus services (until 3am) link Sliema/Paceville with most other parts of the island. This service operates nightly from June to August and at weekends the rest of the year.

Malta's prime tourist strip is a corniche packed with hotels, restaurants, bars and shops, linked by a coastal boardwalk that's also a magnet for Maltese families on summer evenings and weekends.

Development West of Valletta, Sliema sits on the coast at the mouth of Marsamxett Harbour. This strategic position meant it was fortified throughout its history. It's the location of Tigné Fort at the very mouth of the harbour, a *fortizza* at Sliema Point, and was also the position of the second 100-tonne gun to balance the one at Fort Rinella (▷ 58–59), though this fort no longer exists. Sliema is a district of fine period mansions where middle-class Maltese set up home. When tourism grew in the 20th century, its proximity to Valletta made it the sensible choice for hotels, restaurants and bars.

The waterfront At Sliema Creek, the waterfront is home to tour boats offering trips around Grand Harbour (▷ 28–29), and a ferry service for the 10-minute ride across the bay to Valletta. The shopping here is some of the best on the island, with major fashion brands vying for your attention. However, the tourist strip has spread ever westward and now runs continuously from Sliema along the coast. The westward section around St. Julian's (▷ 83) has glossy new five-star hotels and the Portomaso marina. Paceville (pronounced Patch-e-ville) is the bar and nightclub district, where Malta's young and fashionable head.

More to See

The Centre

ATTARD

In the 1620s, Grand Master Antoine de Paule created a luxurious bolthole he named after St. Antony of Padua, his patron saint. St. Anton Palace is now the official residence of the Maltese President. The palace gardens, laid out to plans by de Paule, are open to the public. Tommaso Dingli designed the parish church, dedicated to the Assumption in 1613.

➕ F6 ✉ 7km (4 miles) southwest of Valletta 🚌 40 from Valletta

GĦARGĦUR

One of the least visited villages in Malta, Għargħur gives easy access to the Victoria Lines (▷ 83). The diminutive church of St. Bartholomew, dating from 1610, was originally designed by Tommaso Dingli when he was only 19. The interior is richly baroque in style, with an exceptional ceiling detail. The facade was reworked in the 1730s when the statues of the saints were added. The church owns several fine pieces by Giuseppe Cali (1846–1930), including a vivid canvas—*Martyrdom of St. Bartholomew* (1902)—on the main alter.

➕ F4 ✉ 7km (4 miles) northwest of Valletta 🚌 55, 56 from Valletta

MALTA AVIATION MUSEUM

www.maltaviationmuseum.com

Malta's air force capability during World War II was critical, both for defence of the island and the destruction of Rommel's supply lines to North Africa. This aviation museum restores and displays aircraft that played a pivotal role in the conflict, and other types important to Malta's aviation history. A Supermarine Spitfire, Hawker Hurricane, Douglas DC3, Tiger Moth and Hawker Seahawk are among the prize exhibits.

➕ E6 ✉ Ta' Qali Industrial Estate ☎ 21416095 🕐 Daily 9–5 🍴 Café (€) 🚌 65 from Sliema, 86 from Buġibba ♿ Good 💰 Moderate

San Anton Gardens, Attard

Christian parade at Easter in the streets of Għargħur

MANOEL ISLAND

A small islet in Marsamxett Harbour, joined to the mainland by a short bridge, Manoel was fortified by Grand Master Manoel de Vilhena in 1726 to protect Valletta's western flank. In World War II, the fort was used as a naval base by the British. A programme of considerable refurbishment was completed in 2010.

➕ H5 ✉ Between Valletta and Sliema
🍴 Cafés on Sliema waterfront 🚍 60, 62 from Valletta, 61 from Sliema

MDINA: MDINA DUNGEONS

A series of passages and chambers carved underneath Palazzo Vilhena were formerly used as a prison and torture chamber. A series of modern dioramas feeds the imagination. It's certainly the most gruesome attraction on Malta and not for the squeamish or very young.

➕ D6 ✉ St. Publius Square, Mdina
☎ 21450267 🕐 Daily 9.30–4.30 🍴 Cafés and restaurants nearby 🚍 To Mdina: 80, 81 from Valletta, 65 from Sliema, 86 from Buġibba ♿ Few 💷 Inexpensive

MDINA: PALAZZO FALSON

www.palazzofalson.com

Palazzo Falson is one of the oldest buildings in Mdina. Also known as 'The Norman House', the original elements date from the 13th century, with a second floor added in the 15th century. The 45 collections of documents, utensils, furniture and objets d'art bequeathed by the last owner, Captain Olaf Frederick Gollcher, resonate through the history of Mdina, the Knights of St. John and of Malta.

➕ D6 ✉ Villegaignon Street, Mdina
☎ 21454512 🕐 Tue–Sun 10–7 🍴 Café (€) 🚍 To Mdina: 80, 81 from Valletta, 65 from Sliema, 86 from Buġibba ♿ Good 💷 Expensive

NAXXAR

www.naxxar.com

The name of this town (pronounced Nashaar) translates as 'to hang clothes out to dry' and comes from the legend that St. Paul met some local people here after his shipwreck who tended to him and

Reconstructed medieval kitchen at Palazzo Falson

★

dried his wet clothes. This was one of the 10 original parishes declared on Malta by Bishop de Mello in 1436. Palazzo Parisio (▷ 76) is the prime attraction here, while the grand church dominating the main square is the Church of Our Lady, designed by Tommaso Dingli and completed in 1630. The Church of St. Paul of the Step, where Paul is said to have preached, is 1km (0.6 miles) from the centre of town.

🚹 F5 ✉ 9km (5.5 miles) west of Valletta 🍴 Cafés 🚌 49 (night service), 54, 56 from Valletta

QORMI

Qormi (pronounced Ormi) was given its city charter in 1743. The Maltese knew the town as 'Casal Fornaro' or 'Village of Bakers'. It's now the second largest municipality on the island. The heart of the town is an old quarter of narrow alleyways that's worth exploring. St. George's Church, completed in 1684, dominates the site. The Good Friday procession through town is one of the biggest on Malta where life-sized statues in scenes from the life of Christ are paraded through the streets.

🚹 G6 ✉ 4km (2.5 miles) southwest of Valletta 🍴 Cafés 🚌 88, 89, 91 from Valletta

RABAT

Rabat (along with Mdina, ▷ 72–73) was the location of the Roman capital Melita. Under Arab rule Mdina was fortified, leaving Rabat at the mercy of raiders. Still, Rabat has many ancient treasures from the Roman and early Christian eras, including St. Paul's and St. Agatha's Catacombs (▷ 77) and Domus Romana (▷ 83). St. Paul's Grotto is a small cave where the saint is said to have taken refuge during his time on Malta in AD60. The grotto received a papal visit from John Paul II in 1990 and from Benedict XVI in April 2010.

🚹 D6 ✉ 11km (6.5 miles) southwest of Valletta 🍴 Restaurants and cafés 🚌 80, 81 from Valletta, 65 from Sliema, 86 from Buġibba

Distinctive architecture in a narrow Rabat street

RABAT: DOMUS ROMANA

www.heritagemalta.org

Discovered just outside the walls of Mdina in 1881, on the site of an Arab burial ground, the remains of this Roman town house, or *domus,* have some of the most intricate ancient mosaic floors in Europe. The detail in the work and the small tesserae used to create the patterns is of the finest workmanship, and indicates the wealth and sophistication of Roman Melita (first century BC to second century AD).

➕ D6 ✉ Museum Esplanade, Rabat ☎ 21454125 🕐 Daily 9–5 🍴 Cafés and restaurants nearby 🚌 80, 81 from Valletta, 65 from Sliema, 86 from Buġibba 🦽 Good 👆 Moderate; multi-site tickets: expensive

ST. JULIAN'S

The coastal inlet of St. Julian's has increasingly been swallowed up by the tourist development expanding west from Sliema (▷ 78) and now forms Malta's luxury hospitality sector. There is a selection of large international five-star hotels, which have been opened during the last decade or so. There are some excellent restaurants and bars along the strand.

➕ G5 ✉ 12km (7 miles) from Valletta 🍴 Cafés and restaurants 🚌 62 (night service), 64, 66, 67, 68, 662, 667, 671 from Valletta, 65 from Mdina/Rabat, 652, 645 from Ċirkewwa, 627 from Three Cities/Marsaxlokk, 49 (night service) from Mosta

VICTORIA LINES

The Great Fault is a natural geological feature that runs across Malta. The Knights took advantage of this higher ground, building a series of defensive towers along the ridge. The British expanded these defences by linking them with a stone wall and parapet. Since these extensive works were completed during the reign of Queen Victoria, they became known as the Victoria Lines.

➕ D5 ✉ Northeast of Mosta, Naxxar and Gharghur 🕐 Open access 🚌 None direct; for bus to the nearest town, see the town information panel 🦽 None 👆 Free

The high-rise waterfront of St. Julian's

ŻEBBUĠ OR ĦAL-ŻEBBUĠ

One of the original ten parishes, the town (pronounced Zebuj) was bestowed with the title Citta Rohan by Grand Master de Rohan-Polduc in 1777. The town name means 'olive' in Maltese and attests to the main crop of the district in times gone by. The parish church of St. Philip of Agira was built in 1632 to a design by the son of Gerolamo Cassar, and expanded later by Tommaso Dingli. The fine silver titular statue is by local sculptor Luigi Fontana. Curiously, although St. Philip's feast day falls on 12 May, in Żebbuġ they celebrate on 2 June.

➕ E6 ✉ 8km (5 miles) southwest of Valletta 🍴 Cafés 🚌 88 from Valletta, 881 (night service) from Paceville

The North

GĦAJN TUFFIEĦA BAY

The red sand that forms one of Malta's finest beaches can be reached only on foot and down a couple of hundred natural steps. There are no facilities here, which tends to mean that only the most intrepid, and those seeking quieter shores, venture beyond nearby Golden Bay (▷ below). In the past, the sheltered waters proved a safe haven for Ottoman ships massing for the Great Siege in 1565—the defensive tower atop the cliffs was erected by Grand Master Lascaris in 1637 to prevent the same thing happening again—and during World War II the bay was used by British naval forces.

➕ B4 ✉ 1km (0.6 miles) from Golden Bay 🚌 47, 52 from Valletta, 652 from Sliema

GOLDEN BAY

A yellow arc of sand backed by grassy dunes and rugged bluffs, Golden Bay is arguably the prettiest beach on Malta. It's also one of the most popular, with a monumental five-star hotel flanking one ridge and a large car park to take visiting vehicles. In summer it's the perfect place to acquire a tan and relax but when onshore winds blow, it's the domain of the kite surfers. Be

A sandy beach sweeps round Għajn Tuffieħa Bay

aware that strong currents are at play out towards the open sea and take heed of the warning flags.

🚩 B4 ☒ 3km (2 miles) west of Mġarr 🍴 Cafés and restaurants 🚌 47, 52 from Valletta, 652 from Sliema 🚹 Few

MAJJISTRAL NATURE AND HISTORY PARK

www.majjistral.org

Incorporating the stretch of coastline from Golden Bay (▷ above) north to Anchor Bay, Malta's first National Park protects some of the island's least managed landscapes. The area incorporates cliffs, the island's most extensive sand dunes and expanses of garrigue (low-growing natural scrubland). Two walking trails help get the best out of the area, and there's a guided walk each Sunday at 10am from May to October.

🚩 B4 ☒ North of Golden Bay 🕐 Open access 🍴 Cafés and restaurants at Golden Bay 🚌 To Golden Bay: 47, 52 from Valletta, 652 from Sliema; to Anchor Bay: 441 from Valletta/Mellieħa 🚹 None 🎫 Free

MELLIEĦA

The town sits on a high bluff above the coast, out of the reach of corsairs and pirates who used to roam the waters around Comino (▷ 96–97). The Sanctuary of Our Lady of Victories in the heart of town is still a popular pilgrimage. Worshippers come to pray at a fresco depicting a Pieta, said to have been painted by St. Luke when he was shipwrecked on Malta with St. Paul. Modern studies have proved the fresco to date from the post-Arab late Byzantine era. The complex dates from the late 16th century, with several periods of expansion; the most recent in the 1840s. The narrow strand of Mellieħa Bay to the north is the longest on Malta. Għadira Nature Reserve, backing the beach, is a wetland and salt marsh, and the island's premier bird sanctuary. There are nature trails.

🚩 C3 ☒ 23km (14 miles) northwest of Valletta 🍴 Cafés and restaurants 🚌 43, 44, 441 from Valletta, 45 from Ċirkewwa, 562, 645 from Sliema, 48 from Buġibba/Ċirkewwa

Golden Bay is a favourite of sun-worshippers

Sanctuary of Our Lady of Victories, Mellieħa

Around the North Coast

The route travels through some stretches of the wildest landscapes on Malta, with far-reaching views from the high points.

DISTANCE: 40km (25 miles)   **ALLOW:** 6–8 hours with stops

START

SLIEMA
✚ H5

1 Follow Tower Road (the coast road) from Sliema to St. Julian's (▷ 83). Once through St. Julian's join route 1, turning right for Mellieħa and St. Paul's Bay.

2 The first stopping point is Għargħur (▷ 80). Turn left at the top of the rise, with Pembroke barracks on your right.

3 Return to the main road (route 1) and turn left, passing Splash and Fun park (▷ 89), and continue towards Mellieħa and St. Paul's Bay. The road hugs the coast as far as Salina Bay.

4 Drive on to Mellieħa (▷ 85), then down the ridge towards Ċirkewwa, stopping perhaps at the sandy beach of Mellieħa Bay, which is 2km (1.2 miles) beyond the town.

END

SLIEMA

8 Travel through Mosta and Naxxar (▷ 81–82), turning right on route 18 through San Gwann before taking the coast road right to Sliema.

7 From Golden Bay take the main road right out of the bay, across country to Zebbiegh, to pick up route 17. Turn left here and the road leads on to Mosta (▷ 75).

6 Retrace your route to Mellieħa. Once back at St. Paul's Bay, turn right at the roundabout and head south to Golden Bay (▷ 84–85) and Għajn Tuffieħa (▷ 84). There's an excellent café at Golden Bay for an afternoon coffee.

5 From the beach, carry on along the main road climbing up Marfa Ridge, where there are excellent views.

Around Mdina

This route leads through the streets of Mdina, allowing you to enjoy the medieval architecture. It passes many main attractions.

DISTANCE: 1km (0.6 miles) **ALLOW:** 2–4 hours with stops

 START

MDINA GATE
➕ D6

1 Immediately through the gate in St. Publius Square, the Mdina Dungeons (▷ 81) are on your immediate right. Next door is Palazzo Vilhena and the Natural History Museum.

2 Cross the square and turn left at Mdina Glass, then first right into Triq Villegaignon. Walk past the Malta National Archives on the right to reach Pjazza San Pawl, St. Paul's Square, with its cathedral (▷ 74).

3 Continue along Triq Villegaignon and turn left down the narrow alley of St. Peter's Street.

4 At the end of St. Peter's Street is Magazine Street, where the ammunition for the city used to be stored. Turn right here and walk on past the Knights of Malta attraction (▷ 89).

 END

MDINA GATE

8 Take the turning on the right into St. Roque Street and follow this around, turning left at St. Dorothy's Convent into the rear of St. Paul's Square. Then, retrace your steps up Triq Villegaignon and back to Medina Gate.

7 At the intersection with Bastion Street, turn right, passing the entrance to Fontanella Café.

6 Take Triq Villegaignon out of the square. Pass Palazzo Falson (▷ 81) and then turn off to the left into Our Saviour Street.

5 Pass along St. Agatha's Esplanade to reach Bastion Square. There are excellent views to be seen from the ramparts here.

Shopping

BRISTOW CERAMICS

www.bristowpotteries.com
You'll be able to choose from a range of well-crafted ceramics with bright patterns and themes in their signature yellow and blue hues, all of which have been made and decorated here at the pottery. Most portable of these are the tiles bearing house numbers, decorated with rays of sunshine to remind you of the Maltese summer.

➕ E6 ✉ Craft Village, Ta'Qali ☎ 21421473 🚌 16 from Sliema

GREENHAND LEATHERCRAFT

As the name suggests, you can find leather goods manufactured by this company, but also a range of Maltese lace, plus figurines and models of the Knights Hospitallers and other 'knight' related souvenir items.

➕ D6 ✉ 28 Villegaignon Street, Mdina (also at 2 Magazine Street, Mdina) ☎ 21454689 🚌 To Mdina: 80, 81 from Valletta, 65 from Sliema, 86 from Buġibba

MDINA GLASS

www.mdinaglass.net
The original Maltese glass company is still producing excellent and unique pieces at their workshop in the Craft Village. With the range of colours to be found in Mdina glass, there's sure to be something to suit your taste.

There are several retail outlets across the island.

➕ E6 ✉ Craft Village, Ta' Qali ☎ 21415786 🚌 16 from Sliema

ROMAN VILLA CENTRE

There's a good range of mass-produced souvenirs at this store opposite Domus Romana (▷ 83). You'll find ceramics, T-shirts and sterling silver. Prices are competitive.

➕ D6 ✉ Museum Esplanade, Rabat ☎ 21454048 🚌 To Mdina: 80, 81 from Valletta, 65 from Sliema, 86 from Buġibba

STONES JEWELLERS

This small and rather old-fashioned shop with its period shopfront sits amid fashion boutiques at the heart of Sliema. You'll find traditional filigree work plus handmade jewellery in gold and silver.

➕ H5 ✉ 76 Tower Road, Sliema ☎ 21340264 🚌 62

TA'QALI

The Ta'Qali Craft Village in the centre of the island brings many artisans and craftspeople together in one place. You can watch different types of traditional souvenirs being made, spend a couple of hours browsing, and there are cafés for a drink and a snack. The Craft Village is well signposted once you have arrived in the Ta'Qali area.

(night service), 64, 66, 67, 68, 662, 667, 671 from Valletta, 65 from Mdina/Rabat, 645, 652 from Ċirkewwa, 627 from Three Cities/Marsaxlokk, 49 (night service) from Mosta

SURPLUS & ADVENTURE

After starting out as a store selling ex-military surplus, the owners have expanded into adventure sports, camping and hunting accessories. For collectors of military memorabilia they are well worth a visit but they stock an excellent range of walking boots, water-proofs and other clothing that's fashion and action, plus items that might be useful for picnics while you're touring around.

➕ E5 ✉ Main Street, Mosta ☎ 21420454 🚌 47, 49 (night service), 52, 58, 59, 159 from Valletta, 427 from Buġibba

TOUCHSTONE

www.touchstoneculture.org
You can while away an hour or so at this gallery and bookshop because it's also a café. Local artists are represented here, and there is some interesting and unique art—painting, sculpture and ceramics—celebrating Maltese themes as well as more abstract pieces.

➕ C3 ✉ Main Street, Mellieħa ☎ 21524451 🚌 43, 44, 441 from Valletta, 45 from Ċirkewwa, 562, 645 from Sliema, 48 from Buġibba/Ċirkewwa

Entertainment and Activities

DRAGONARA CASINO BARRIÈRE ST. JULIAN'S

www.dragonara.com
Malta's first casino is still its most popular and spectacular, set in a 19th-century summer palace.
🔁 G4 ⊠ Dragonara Point, St. Julian's ☎ 21382362
🕐 Mon–Thu 10am–3am, Fri–Sun 24 hours 🚌 62 (night service), 64, 66, 67, 68, 662, 667, 671 from Valletta, 65 from Mdina/Rabat, 645, 652 from Ćirkewwa, 627 from Three Cities/Marsaxlokk, 49 (night service) from Mosta

HAVANA CLUB

www.havanamalta.com
One of the entertainment district's coolest night-clubs, this is a prime spot for soul, hip-hop and R&B sounds, as well as music from the 1960s to the 1990s, depending on the evening.
🔁 G4 ⊠ St. George's Road, St. Julian's ☎ 21374500
🕐 Daily 9pm–late 🚌 62 (night service), 64, 66, 67, 68, 662, 667, 671 from Valletta, 65 from Mdina/Rabat, 645, 652 from Ćirkewwa, 627 from Three Cities/Marsaxlokk, 49 (night service) from Mosta

GOLDEN BAY HORSE RIDING STABLES

This is a well-run stables, whether you want to learn to ride or you're an experienced rider and fancy a canter through the Maltese countryside.
🔁 B4 ⊠ Golden Bay, Mellieħa ☎ 21573360
🕐 May–Sep daily 7am–9pm; Oct–Apr 9–5 🚌 47, 52 from Valletta, 652 from Sliema

THE KNIGHTS OF MALTA

www.theknightsofmalta.com
A walk-though attraction with dioramas depicting the life and times of the Hospitaller Knights, complete with relevant sounds and aromas for extra authenticity.
🔁 D6 ⊠ 14–19 Casa Magazzini, Magazine Street, Mdina ☎ 21451342 🕐 Daily 10–5 🚌 To Mdina: 80, 81 from Valletta, 65 from Sliema, 86 from Buġibba

THE MDINA EXPERIENCE

www.themdinaexperience.com
A large-screen film extravaganza depicting the major events in the long history of The Silent City.
🔁 D6 ⊠ 7 Mesquita Square, Mdina ☎ 21450055 🕐 Daily 10–5 🚌 To Mdina: 80, 81 from Valletta, 65 from Sliema, 86 from Buġibba

CASINO ETIQUETTE

The age limit for entry into casinos in Malta is 18 for non-Maltese and 25 for Maltese nationals. Dress code is smart casual so ties are not compulsory, but you certainly won't be allowed in wearing shorts or anything that resembles beachwear. Take your passport or some form of photo-ID, in case you need proof of identity and age.

MEDIEVAL TIMES

This walk-through attraction depicts daily life for people in the Mdina of the Middle Ages.
🔁 D6 ⊠ Palazzo Costanzo, Villegaignon Street, Mdina ☎ 21454625 🕐 Mon–Sat 10–4.30 🚌 To Mdina: 80, 81 from Valletta, 65 from Sliema, 86 from Buġibba

MEDITERRANEO MARINE PARK

www.marineparkmalta.com
The main attraction here is the 'Swim with the Dolphins' experience (over 8s only).
🔁 F4 ⊠ Coast Road, Baħar iċ-Ċagħaq ☎ 21378781
🕐 Mar–Oct daily 10–5 🚌 68 from Valletta, 70, 652 from Sliema/Buġibba

POPEYE VILLAGE

www.popeyemalta.com
The set for the film Popeye (1980) is now a lively theme park, with shows and animation.
🔁 B3 ⊠ Anchor Bay, Mellieħa ☎ 2152782
🕐 Apr–Sep daily 9.30–5.30; Oct–Mar 9.30–4.30 🚌 441 from Valletta/Mellieħa

SPLASH AND FUN WATERPARK

www.splashandfun.com.mt
Malta's only waterpark has a range of rides and flumes, including The Black Hole and the Drift Away Lazy River.
🔁 F4 ⊠ Coast Road, Baħar iċ-Ċagħaq ☎ 21374283
🕐 May–Oct daily 9–7 🚌 68 from Valletta, 70, 652 from Sliema/Buġibba

THE CENTRE AND THE NORTH

ENTERTAINMENT AND ACTIVITIES

Restaurants

PRICES

Prices are approximate, based on a 3-course meal for one person.

€€€   over €30
€€   €20–€30
€   under €20

FAT HARRY'S (€)

www.fatharryspub.com
The liveliest theme pub in St. Paul's Bay sells hearty pub-style grub including steaks, roast chicken and a mean plate of fish and chips.

➕ E3 ✉ Bay Square, Buġibba ☎ 21572163 🕐 Daily 11am–late 🚌 49, 58, 59, 159 from Valletta, 70, 652 from Sliema, 86 from Mdina/Rabat

FONTANELLA TEA GARDEN (€)

This pretty café has a terrace with extensive views down from the city walls of Mdina. The rich chocolate cake is a specialty to enjoy.

➕ D6 ✉ 1 Bastion Street, Mdina ☎ 21450208 🕐 Jun–Sep daily 10am–11pm; Oct–May Mon–Fri 10–6, Sat–Sun 10–10 🚌 80, 81 from Valletta, 65 from Sliema 86 from Buġibba

GIUSEPPI'S WINE BAR (€€–€€€)

www.giuseppismalta.com
Giuseppi's has a warm and welcoming, formal, trattoria-style interior and a menu that changes with what's fresh in season. Try the quail and rabbit in chocolate sauce, or the deep-fried Gozitan goat's cheese if on the menu.

➕ C3 ✉ G Borg Olivier Street, Mellieħa ☎ 21574882 🕐 Mon–Sat dinner 🚌 43, 44, 441 from Valletta, 45 from Ċirkewwa, 562, 645 from Sliema, 48 from Buġibba/Ċirkewwa

MADLIENA COTTAGE BRASSERIE (€€–€€€)

This traditional farmhouse has been transformed into a lovely restaurant that's worth seeking out for a dinner to dress for. Enjoy live jazz music on Wednesdays.

➕ F4 ✉ Triqil-Bir, Madliena ☎ 21580866 🕐 May–Sep daily dinner; Oct–Apr Mon–Sat dinner, Sun lunch and dinner 🚌 None

THE MEDINA (€€€)

In this vaulted stone mansion the Mediterranean menu is presented in ultra-contemporary style.

➕ D6 ✉ 7 Holy Cross Street, Mdina ☎ 21454004 🕐 Mon–Sat dinner 🚌 80, 81 from Valletta, 65 from Sliema 86 from Buġibba

FINE DINING

For fine dining, try Le Mondion restaurant (€€€; tel 21450560; Mon–Sat dinner) at the Xara Palace Hotel, Mdina (▷ 112). Executive chef Kevin Bonello has been rewarded with the accolade Maltese Chef of the Year (2009) for his delicious 'modern Mediterranean' cuisine.

TA'KRIS (€–€€)

This Maltese restaurant serves excellent local cuisine in a warm trattoria atmosphere, and it doesn't break the bank.

➕ H5 ✉ 80 Fawwara Lane, Sliema ☎ 21337367 🕐 Daily lunch and dinner 🚌 62 (night service), 64, 66, 67, 68, 662, 667, 671 from Valletta, 65 from Mdina/Rabat, 645, 652 from Ċirkewwa, 627 from Three Cities/Marsaxlokk, 49 (night service) from Mosta

TRATTORIA AD1530 (€–€€)

www.xarapalace.com.mt
A typically short trattoria menu of daily specials is served in a rustic dining room, or outside in a quiet square. Try the Maltese platter of cheeses and charcuterie.

➕ D6 ✉ Xara Palace Hotel, Misrah il-Kunsill, Mdina ☎ 21450560 🕐 Daily lunch and dinner 🚌 80, 81 from Valletta, 65 from Sliema, 86 from Buġibba

VECCHIA NAPOLI (€)

www.vecchianapoli.com
This excellent no-nonsense pizza and pasta place has quick service and quaffable bottles of house wine.

➕ G5 ✉ Tower Road, Sliema ☎ 21343434 🕐 Mon–Fri dinner, Sat–Sun lunch and dinner 🚌 62 (night service), 64, 66, 67, 68, 662, 667, 671 from Valletta; 65 from Mdina/Rabat; 652, 645 from Ċirkewwa; 627 from Three Cities/Marsaxlokk; 49 (night service) from Mosta

Malta's smaller siblings present a very different face to the world. On Gozo, traditions are strong and nature still reigns. It's an island where hiking and diving are the major draws. Tiny Comino is home to one of the Mediterranean's most picturesque vistas—the Blue Lagoon.

Ir-Ramla

ergla

Ta' Venuta

Ta' Gajdoru

Il-Bajja
ta' San Blas

Ghajn
Hosna

Mistra Rocks
(Gebel Mistra)

I-Ghajjun

Ta' Spilotti

Dahlet
Qorrot

Ta' Sardina

Bin Gemma

Ta' Cini

Ta' Tocc

Ta' Hida

Ta' Muxi

15

Il-Wilga

Nadur

15

Qala

Il-Qasam

Ta' Bordin

Ta' Kusbejja

Tan-Nemes

Qala Point (Ras il-Qala)

Wardija

Hondoq

Mrejzbiet

Iz-Zewwieqa

ir-Rummien

Ta' Xilep

Ghajnsielem

Mgarr

Hondoq
Bay

Il-Fliegu Ta' Ghawdex

Floriana/Valletta

Ta' Brieghen

Port ta' l-Imgarr

Il-Bajja ta
San Niklaw

Il-Bajja ta'
Santa
Marija

garr
Xini
Bay

Il-Ponta tal-Mellieha

Blue Lagoon
(Bejn il-Kmiemen)

Comino
(Kemmuna)

Cominotto
(Kemmunett)

Wied Ternu
Bay

Il-Fliegu ta' Malta

D

E

F

Azure Window & Fungus Rock

The power of wind and waves over rock is writ large in this monumental natural feature. It's one of Gozo's most dramatic landscapes and it's one of its most photographed sights.

Azure Window Gozo's northwestern coast is characterized by a ribbon of vertiginous cliffs, but the Azure Window, easily accessible by foot and by boat, has become the totem for the island's coastal-scapes. A natural arch formed by millennia of erosion, the feature gets its name—Tieqa Zerqa, or Azure Window—from the hue of the surrounding water. The Azure Window can be viewed easily from the flanking rocks, but the boat trip under the arch from the nearby Dwejra Inland Sea (▷ 101), is a popular hour-long excursion.

Fungus Rock The nub of rock jutting 60m (196ft) out of the sea just offshore, and to the west of the Azure Window, is Fungus Rock. It is so called because a particular plant—*Cynomorium coccineum* (actually a parasitic rhizome, not a fungus)—was found growing here. The Knights believed it had healing properties and it became an important medicine for the treatment of dysentery, ulcers and fatigue. It was so prized that samples of the plant would often be given as gifts to noble families and other benefactors, and it became known around Europe as the Maltese Mushroom. Dwejra Tower, constructed by the Knights on the mainland opposite the rock, is an indication of the lengths they went to in order to protect this valuable asset. Anyone found trespassing on the rock would have been severely punished.

THE BASICS

➕ AIII
✉ San Lawrenz, Gozo
🕐 Open access (boat trips from Dwejra Inland Sea: May–Oct daily 9am–dusk, weather permitting)
🍴 Cafés and restaurants open May–Oct; refreshment stand open all year
🚌 91 from Victoria
♿ None
💷 Free; boat trips: expensive

Comino

HIGHLIGHTS

● The Blue Lagoon, for photographs, snorkelling and diving
● Walking over the garrigue
● Peace and tranquillity

TIPS

● If you want a day on Comino walking, hiking or bird watching, book the hotel boat or private boat transfer.
● Don't forget sunscreen, sunglasses, hat and insect repellent, to guard against sunburn and pests.

One of the Mediterranean's finest natural playgrounds, Comino and its coastal shallows offer acres of wild countryside and limpid waters that are a paradise for those who love the outdoors.

History The smallest of the Maltese islands, Comino lies sandwiched between Malta and Gozo in the Gozo Channel. It is named after the cumin seeds that used to be grown here. Inhabited during Roman times, Comino became a pirate stronghold in the Middle Ages. The Knights used it as a hunting ground—for hares and wild boar—and later as a place of exile. Today it's a bird sanctuary.

Away from it all Comino offers the chance to escape the bustle of 21st-century life. There are

The azure hue of The Blue Lagoon is caused by sunlight reflecting on the sand under the water (left); the fishing port of St. Paul's Bay is the embarkation point for cruises to Comino (right)

no cars here and visitor numbers are limited by the boat traffic. There are few buildings; St. Mary's Tower, built in 1618, is the most prominent. Comino Hotel (tel 21529821; www.cominohotel.com; open summer only) at St. Niklaw Bay has several eateries, ranging from snack bars to an à la carte restaurant. Alternatively, bring a picnic.

The Blue Lagoon Lying in the shallows between Comino and the islet of Cominetto, The Blue Lagoon is one of the Mediterranean's most incredible watery spectacles. The sun reflecting from the sable sand gives the whole bay an iridescent azure glow. This is Malta's premier diving and snorkelling spot, and it's a favourite location for film crews. Many of the naval scenes in *Troy* (2004) were filmed here.

Ġgantija

TOP
25

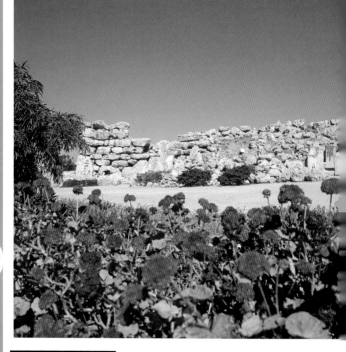

DID YOU KNOW?

● The name Ġgantija comes from the word *ġgant*, meaning giant. In a Gozitan legend, a female giant carried the stones on her back and placed them here.

TIP

● There's a stand just by the ticket office selling home-made honey and fruit in season. All the produce comes from the farmland immedi-ately around the temple site. It is all organic, and delicious!

It doesn't look much now, but this was the earliest known man-made structure in the world. Built by a sophisticated civilization lost to history, Ġgantija kick-started our love affair with architecture.

History Ġgantija (pronounced jgan-teeya) was started c.3600BC and was in use for 1,000 years, until the sudden disappearance of the Temple Building civilization. Thought to be the centre of a fertility cult, it later became a cer-emonial cremation site. Ġgantija was uncovered in 1820 but wasn't properly studied until 1933.

The temple today Set on an artificial plateau with panoramic views across the countryside, the coralline stonework comprises rough-hewn blocks. It's a complex of two temples within an

The ruins of the Ġgantija temples, thought to be the oldest free-standing monuments in the world (left); massive coralline limestone walls surround uprights topped with lintel stones (top right); a temple entrance (bottom right)

outer wall rising to 6m (20ft) in height. Each temple has a separate single entryway. The larger, more southerly, temple is the earlier, at c.3600BC, and comprises five semi-circular apses fanning out from a central corridor. Holes in the stone portals suggest doors once separated the outer area from the inner sanctum. Libation holes in the floors are thought to be where the blood of sacrifices flowed away. The complex portals have finer stonework than the walls, but still not as fine as the later temples of Tarxien (▷ 54–55) and Ħaġar Qim (▷ 49).

Xaghra Stone Circle Close by is a collapsed series of ancient funerary chambers. Human remains have been found, the earliest of which dates from around 4000BC. It is believed that the circle was related to activities at Ġgantija.

THE BASICS

www.heritagemalta.org

✚ CIII

✉ Xaghra village, Gozo

☎ 21553194

🕐 Daily 9–7 (last admission 4.30)

🍴 Cafés within walking distance

🚌 To Xaghra: 64, 65 from Victoria

♿ None

💷 Moderate

Gozo Citadel

Victoria Cathedral in the Citadel (left); the Citadel battlements (right)

THE BASICS

www.heritagemalta.org

✚ CIII

✉ Victoria, Gozo

☎ Museums: 21556144

🕓 Museums: daily 9–5

🍴 Cafés and restaurants within the Citadel

🚌 None direct

♿ Few

💲 Individual museums: inexpensive; combined ticket for all museums: moderate

❓ Self-guided audiotour

DID YOU KNOW?

● When the Knights of St. John vanquished the Ottomans and reclaimed the Citadel, they issued an edict that all Gozitans should retreat behind the walls at night to ensure their safety. This practice continued for almost 100 years.

TIP

● Magnificent views of the surrounding countryside are seen from the walls.

This tiny fortified enclave was the island capital for many centuries and it is still the seat of the island's bishop. Today, it has some fine medieval architecture and a collection of good museums.

Echoes of the past Inhabitation of the site goes back to the Roman era but the strategic value of this high ground was realized by the Arabs, then the European nobility who took control of Gozo. The small enclave was well fortified but not enough to withstand the Ottoman attack of 1551, when the walls were breached, the buildings razed and many Gozitans taken into servitude. After the Great Siege on Malta, the Knights of St. John strengthened the enclave. The Citadel was badly damaged in an earthquake in 1693 but it rose again until Victoria (Rabat) grew up outside the walls in modern times. Today, there are only a few full-time residents.

What to see The most imposing building is Gozo's cathedral (▷ 101), whose facade faces visitors as they arrive through the main gateway into the Citadel. The Citadel museums host an eclectic mix of exhibitions: The Archaeology Museum has artefacts from Ġgantija Temple, along with Roman and Phoenician finds; the Folklore Museum shows historic arts and crafts; the Old Prison built by the Knights in 1548 houses an exhibition on forts; and the Museum of Natural Science displays fossils, stuffed birds and preserved insects.

More to See

DWEJRA INLAND SEA
This large lagoon is separated from the open sea but connected to it by a narrow tunnel, 60m (196ft) through limestone cliffs. During the summer, small boats take trips through the tunnel to view the Azure Window (▷ 94).

➕ AIII ✉ Qawra, San Lawrenz, Gozo ⏲ Open access; boat trips: Easter–Oct daily 9–dusk, weather permitting 🍴 Cafés and restaurants May–Oct; refreshment stand open all year 🚌 91 from Victoria ♿ None 💷 Free to view; boat trips: expensive

TA'PINU CHURCH
www.tapinu.org
Built between 1920 and 1931, Ta'Pinu is revered as a church of miracles. Inside the neo-Gothic edifice you can read touching stories of those who believe their prayers have been answered.

➕ BIII ✉ Ta'Pinu, just southeast of Gharb, Gozo ☎ 21556187 ⏲ Mon–Sat 6.30–12.15, 1.30–7, Sun 5.45–12.15, 1.30–7 🚌 91 from Victoria (but not all services) ♿ Good 💷 Free

VICTORIA: CATHEDRAL
www.gozocathedral.org.mt
Designed by Lorenzo Gafà, and completed in 1711, the interior has many fine baroque details. The limestone floor comprises hundreds of ornate tombstones of Gozitan nobility and clergy. The dome is a trompe l'oeil.

➕ CIII ✉ The Citadel, Victoria, Gozo ☎ 21554101 ⏲ Mon–Sat 10–1, 1.30–4.30 🍴 Cafés and restaurants in the Citadel 🚌 None direct ♿ Few 💷 Inexpensive

VICTORIA: ST. GEORGE'S CHURCH
www.stgeorge.org.mt
Behind a 19th-century facade this is glorious baroque (1672), designed by Vittorio Cassar, and enhanced by an altarpiece credited to Mattia Preti. The baldachin (altar canopy) was inspired by the Bernini baldachin in St. Peter's Church, Rome.

➕ CIII ✉ St. George's Square, Victoria, Gozo ☎ 21556377 ⏲ Daily 4.30–1, 3.30–7 🍴 Cafés in the square 🚌 None direct ♿ Few 💷 Free

The neo-Gothic church of Ta'Pinu, on Gozo

Around Gozo

This drive takes in a good range of Gozo's attractions and landscapes, allowing you to get a real feel for the island.

DISTANCE: 13km (8 miles) **ALLOW:** 6–8 hours with stops

START

MGARR FERRY TERMINAL
➕ DIV

1 From the ferry follow signs, right for Nadur, at the intersection with the Victoria road. Follow this uphill for 1km (0.6 miles), then turn right to Qala.

2 After 1.25km (0.8 miles), you'll reach Qala with its ruined windmills. Turn left through the village and continue to Nadur, where there is a packed private Maritime Museum.

3 Leave Nadur on the route to Victoria (route 2), and after 2.75km (1.7 miles) turn right on route 4, towards Xagħra. Look for a sign, right, to Ġgantija Temple (▷ 98–99).

4 From the temple, turn right and travel into Xagħra village. Turn right at the village square and then left after 300m (330 yards), taking the back route signposted Marsalforn.

END

AZURE WINDOW
➕ AIII

8 At the intersection with route 1, turn right towards St. Lawrence/Dwejra and continue to the Azure Window (▷ 94).

7 From the church car park, turn left into Gharb. Turn left at the church square, where there is a fascinating Folk Museum. Follow the road 0.5km (0.3 miles) back towards Victoria.

6 Follow the road and you'll see Ta'Pinu church (▷ 101) on the right. Take the narrow road to the church after 3km (1.9 miles).

5 Leave Marsalforn along the main route to Victoria (route 3), climbing up into the capital. At the main intersection in Victoria turn right, signposted San Lawrenz/St. Lawrence (route 1). The Citadel is on your right.

Shopping

BASTION LACE

Maria Mizzi sells an extensive selection of handmade Gozitan lace—she may even be at work on her bobbins when you call—so this is the place to come to compare prices and sizes, and to get some good advice.

🕂 CIII ✉ Bieb il-Imdina Street, Citadel, Victoria, Gozo ☎ 21561471 🚌 None direct

FONTANA CRAFTS

On the Xlendi Road out of Victoria, this old washhouse built by the Hospitallers is now a craft centre, selling local hand-produced, and some mass-produced, items. It's a good place to browse for and buy all your Gozitan souvenirs.

🕂 BIV ✉ Ghajn Tuta Street, Fontana, Gozo ☎ 21553726 🚌 87 from Victoria

GOZO GLASS

www.gozoglass.com.mt Gozo Glass has been in business since 1989, and is family owned and operated. The glassworks produces hand-blown designs featuring traditional styles and patterns, plus modern ranges with hues from vivid marine blue to earthy deep pinks and browns.

🕂 BIII ✉ 9 Gharb Road, Gharb, Gozo ☎ 21561974 🚌 1, 2, 91 from Victoria

JOE XUEREB

www.joexuereb.com This Gozo-born sculptor takes local stone and carves it into the most beautiful pieces that would grace any household. Taking his inspiration from the ancient priest-ess figures found across Malta, he excels at capturing the characteristic soft curved forms. Xuereb has an impressive list of exhibitions of his work held at locations around the world.

🕂 DIV ✉ 'Ta' Peppi', Bahhara Street, Ghajnsielem, Gozo ☎ 21553559 🚌 To Ghajnsielem village: 42, 43 from Victoria

JUBILEE FOODS

www.jubileefoods.net Beautifully packaged local foods, including island-produced extra virgin olive oil, honey, cheese, capers and sea salt, are sold here. You can taste many of the products before you buy. Jubilee Foods also package their own excellent frozen pasticcio and other Maltese pastas, as well as dried pastas.

🕂 CIII ✉ Independence Square, Victoria, Gozo ☎ 21558921 🚌 None direct

ROSANNA'S CRAFT SHOP

There's a comprehensive range of souvenirs and unusual gifts on offer in a shop that seems packed to the rafters. Best buys include knitwear and textiles, glass, lace and ceramics. There is something for every budget—even items for children's pocket money.

🕂 AIII ✉ Shop 2, Ta'Dbiegi Craft Village, San Lawrenz, Gozo ☎ 21555139 🚌 1, 2, 91 from Victoria

TA'DOLINO

This small shop, close to St. George's Church, sells a range of sterling silver souvenirs and gifts. Many have religious themes for local weddings, communions and baptisms.

🕂 CIII ✉ St. George's Square, Victoria, Gozo ☎ 21551130 🚌 None direct

TA'RIKARDU

Set in a lovely vaulted mansion in the heart of the Citadel, this restaurant-cum-shop sells a range of Gozitan edibles and wines, and some interesting locally produced one-of-a-kind ceramics.

🕂 CIII ✉ 4 Fosos Street, Citadel, Victoria, Gozo ☎ 21555953 🚌 None direct

TA'DBIEGI CRAFTS

The Ta'Dbiegi Craft Village, close to San Lawrenz in the west of the island, is a district specially designated for artisans producing and selling Gozitan crafts. There's an excellent range on offer including blown glass, ceramics, lace, leather goods and knitwear. You can even watch the craftspeople at work making the items on show and chat to them about the techniques involved.

Entertainment and Activities

GOZO 360°

This 30-minute film tells the story of Gozo and takes viewers on an aerial tour around the island. It's a visual spectacular that brings many facets of Gozitan life into focus in a short space of time.

🕇 CIII ⊠ Citadel Theatre, Castle Hill, Victoria, Gozo ☎ 21559955 🕐 Mon–Sat 10.30–3.30, Sun 10.30–1. Shows start on the hour and half hour 🚌 None direct

GOZO ADVENTURES

www.gozoadventures.com
Gozo Adventures is a well-established company offering a variety of guided sports to help you get the best out of the island. In addition to boat trips, hiking and diving, they offer sports climbing, coasteering (following routes along the water's edge and around cliffs) and abseiling.

🕇 CIII ⊠ Head Office: 7 Triq Indrija, Victoria, Gozo ☎ 21564592 🕐 All year; some activities are seasonal 🚌 None direct

GOZO PRIDE TOURS

www.gozopridetours.com
This tour company offers a range of full- and half-day tours, from straightforward island itineraries by mini-bus to jeep safaris and quad-bike adventures. They'll take you overland or on the water.

🕇 EIV ⊠ Head Office: 27 Anton Buttigieg Street, Qala, Gozo ☎ 21564776 🕐 All

year; some activities seasonal 🚌 To Qala: 42, 43 from Victoria

LA GROTTA NIGHTCLUB

www.lagrottaleisure.com
Covering several caves and terraces cascading down the ravine just outside Xlendi, La Grotta blasts into the night during the summer.

🕇 BIV ⊠ Xlendi Road, Xlendi, Gozo ☎ 21551149 🕐 May–Oct Fri–Sat 9pm–late 🚌 87 (daytime only) from Victoria

KEMPINSKI SPA

www.kempinski.com
Specializing in Ayurveda (traditional Indian wellness regime) techniques, the spa also offers more than 40 other treatments. If you want to learn yoga, pilates or aquarobics, or you want to improve your technique there are qualified instructors on site.

OUT AND ABOUT

Gozo is considered one of the Mediterranean's best locations for outdoor activities of all kinds. The *Gozo Adventures Handbook* by Xavier Hancock (ISBN-10: 99932-0-469-2) has been produced with the cooperation of the Tourist Office, leading adventure companies and others, to showcase locations for each activity. It's available from the Malta Tourist Authority (▷ 120).

🕇 AIII ⊠ Triq il-Rokon, San Lawrenz, Gozo ☎ 22110000 🕐 Daily 8–8 🚌 1, 2, 91 from Victoria

MOBY DIVES

www.mobydivesgozo.com
This PADI five-star accredited dive centre runs everything from children's introductions to diving, to Dive Master and Master Scuba Diver standard.

🕇 BIV ⊠ Xlendi Bay, Gozo ☎ 21554606 🕐 May–Oct 🚌 87 from Victoria

VICTOR MUSCAT HORSE RIDING

www.vmcarriages.com
Enjoy hacking in the Gozo countryside or through the waves at Ramla Bay. Victor also offers carriage tours, so you can see the island at a leisurely pace.

🕇 CIII ⊠ Shaft Street, Xaghra, Gozo ☎ 21559229 🕐 All year by appointment 🚌 To Xaghra: 64, 65 from Victoria

XLENDI PLEASURE CRUISES

www.xlendicruises.com
With this family-owned company you can choose from a range of pleasure trips around Gozo, including the Azure Window, or head out to Comino for the day and swim in the Blue Lagoon (▷ 97). Free transport is available from Marsalforn and Xlendi to Mġarr Harbour.

🕇 DIV ⊠ Head Office: Bakery Street, Marsalforn, Gozo ☎ 99478119 🕐 Apr–Oct 🚌 21 from Victoria

Restaurants

PRICES

Prices are approximate, based on a 3-course meal for one person.
€€€ over €30
€€ €20–€30
€ under €20

BONITO'S (€€€)

www.gozorestaurant.com
There's a tempting array of Mediterranean cuisine at this respected restaurant in the heart of Xlendi. Steaks from Argentina, and locally caught fish.
➕ BIV ✉ Triq il-Madonna tel-Karmnu, Xlendi, Gozo ☎ 21559315 🕐 Apr–Dec daily lunch and dinner; Jan–Mar Fri–Sun lunch and dinner 🚌 87 from Victoria

CAFÉ JUBILEE (€)

www.cafejubilee.com
This small 1920s-style pub is a great place for a drink and a meal at any time of the year. Daily specials are on the chalkboard and Jubilee Foods renowned pasta makes a good choice.
➕ CIII ✉ Independence Square, Victoria, Gozo ☎ 21558921 🕐 Kitchen hours daily 8–3, 6–10; pub open Sun–Thu 8am–midnight, Fri–Sat 8am–2am 🚌 None direct

COUNTRY TERRACE LOUNGE BAR & RESTAURANT (€€)

www.country-terrace.com
The extensive terrace with views looking down to the Gozo Channel is a lovely place for seafood and game. There are BBQ nights in the summer and a Sunday lunch buffet.
➕ DIV ✉ Zewwieqa Street, Mġarr, Gozo ☎ 21550248 🕐 Daily lunch and dinner 🚌 To Mġarr: 42, 43 from Victoria

IT'TMUN WINE BAR & LOUNGE (€€)

www.tmunvictoria.com
The Mediterranean-French menu at It'Tmun is served in a classy bistro and cool lounge. The wine list is extensive, with both local and international labels. It's popular with Gozitans.
➕ CIII ✉ Europe Street, Victoria, Gozo ☎ 21566667 🕐 Fri–Wed dinner 🚌 None direct

IL-KARTELL (€–€€)

www.il-kartellrestaurant.com
At this respected restaurant, seafood and pasta are delicious. In summer there is live music on some evenings.
➕ CII ✉ Main Street, Marsalforn, Gozo

ĠBEJNIET CHEESE

Don't forget to try gbejniet (Gozo cheese) during your stay. When it's fresh it has a white hue, soft consistency and a slightly tart taste that can accompany savoury and sweet items. As it ages, it becomes harder in texture and stronger in taste—wonderful with the charcuterie and wine produced on Gozo.

☎ 21275569/21556918 🕐 May–Oct daily lunch and dinner; Nov–Apr Mon–Fri lunch, Sat–Sun lunch and dinner 🚌 87 from Victoria

TA'FRENC (€€€)

www.tafrencrestaurant.com
Ta'Frenc offers dishes flambéed at the table, as well as hand-reared chickens and home-grown herbs as ingredients throughout all their Gozitan-inspired dishes.
➕ CIII ✉ Ghajn Damma Street (on the way to Marsalforn), Gozo ☎ 21553883 🕐 May–Oct Wed–Mon lunch and dinner; Nov–Apr Sat–Sun lunch and dinner 🚌 21 from Victoria

TA'RIKARDU (€)

Set in a vaulted mansion in the heart of the Citadel, this restaurant-cum-shop has long wooden tables and limestone walls. Daily Gozitan specials include rabbit and ravioli, accompanied by local wines.
➕ CIII ✉ 4 Fosos Street, Citadel, Victoria, Gozo ☎ 21555953 🕐 Daily lunch and dinner 🚌 None direct

ZAFIRO (€€)

www.hotelsanandrea.com
This pretty waterside restaurant is at Hotel San Andrea. It offers a mouth-watering finely sliced beef in wine with onions and ginger.
➕ BIV ✉ Xlendi waterfront, Gozo ☎ 21565555 🕐 Daily lunch and dinner 🚌 87 from Victoria

RESTAURANTS

GOZO & COMINO

Malta and Gozo have a good choice of accommodation in all price brackets, ranging from vast beach resorts to small family-run establishments. The quality of provision reflects recent investment.

Where to Stay

Introduction

Malta has always been a popular place for package tourists but in recent years, especially with the increase in choice of airlines flying to the island, it's become much easier to tailor-make your own trip.

Malta Accommodation

The major pockets of accommodation are all on the north coast, with the large, luxury properties generally concentrated around St. Julian's Bay, and more mid-range options around the longer-established resort of Sliema, and in the St. Paul's Bay/Qawra area farther away from the capital. Malta doesn't have many sandy beaches, so if this is important to you, head to Mellieħa Bay or Golden Bay. Along the Sliema/ St. Julian's strip, sunbathing and bathing is from rocky lidos. Most luxury hotels are large and backed by international names. Boutique hotels are few but they are making their mark and the quality is excellent.

Gozo Accommodation

Gozo has fewer hotels than Malta and they are generally smaller in size. This doesn't mean that quality suffers, however. In fact, the two five-star properties are always in the running for the island's best hotel prize. Marsalforn, Xlendi and Mġarr all have a choice of options in the budget to mid-range price bracket. Check ahead, since hotels are more likely to close in winter (approximately November to March) on Gozo, as the island is much quieter than Malta at this time of year. Self-catering options, such as apartment or farmhouse rentals, are a more popular choice on this island, and there is a good range to choose from.

SEASONAL SURPRISES

Prices in this guide relate to summer season (generally April to October) rates but there are always bargains to be had during the rest of the year because competition is fierce. A bit of research beforehand means you may be able to afford a far better class of hotel on your late- or early-season break than you thought!

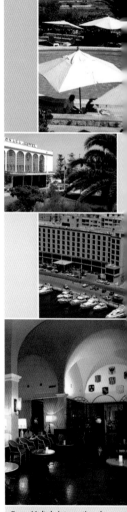

From Malta's international luxury hotels to Gozo's farmhouses, there is something for everyone

Budget Hotels

Malta

ASTI PENSIONE

This 350-year-old former priory, complete with original features, makes a comfortable family-run guest house. Rooms differ in size and decoration. One bathroom on each floor caters for every couple of rooms. There's a small breakfast room on the ground floor.

🔲 d3 ✉ 18 St. Ursula Street, Valletta ☎ 21239506

THE BRITISH HOTEL

www.britishhotel.com
The longest-established hotel in Valletta has an excellent location, with most rooms overlooking Grand Harbour. Rooms tend to be compact and simply furnished but are good value. A restaurant, summer terrace and TV room complete the hotel's facilities.

🔲 d3 ✉ 40 Battery Street, Valletta ☎ 21224730

CASTILLE HOTEL

www.hotelcastillemalta.com
This three-star property, set in a former palace, offers pleasant and comfortable accommodation with lovely touches in the period-style furnishings. Rooms have TV and WiFi. The De Robertis

restaurant on the top floor has exceptional views across the city and Grand Harbour. The La Cave cellar pizzeria/wine bar is also popular.

🔲 d3 ✉ Castille Square, Valletta ☎ 21243677

GRAND HARBOUR HOTEL

www.grandharbourhotel.com
Overlooking Grand Harbour, with a roof terrace and lounge with panoramic window to watch the comings and goings of shipping, this hotel offers basic but good value accommodation. There's a bar and restaurant on site.

🔲 d3 ✉ 47 Battery Street, Valletta ☎ 21246003

HOTEL PLEVNA

www.plevnahotel.com
A mid-sized hotel set in a residential street a two-minute walk from the Sliema waterfront, the Plevna's bright and modern interior gives an airy feel and the rooms have rustic wooden furniture. There's a sun terrace on site but the hotel also

has a summer seaside beach club (May–Oct) with a seawater pool, sun beds, snack bar, lido, sea access and a changing area.

🔲 H5 ✉ Hughes Mallett Street, Sliema ☎ 21331031

POINT DE VUE

www.pointdevuemalta.com
A neoclassical mansion that's been in the hotel business since 1898. Today, it's a well-run guest house with well-furnished rooms at an excellent price, with a café, internet café and a good restaurant on site. It's an excellent option if you don't need a beach resort setting to make or break your holiday.

🔲 D6 ✉ 5 Saqqajja, Rabat ☎ 21454117

Gozo

MARIA GIOVANNA GUEST HOUSE

www.tamariagozo.com
A Gozitan town house in the heart of Marsalforn, offering 21st-century perks like air-conditioning and an elevator combined with period features, such as traditional tiled floors and local wooden furniture. Small modern bathrooms have been installed in each room. The website has information about a range of accommodation offered by the owners, including luxury Gozitan farmhouses.

🔲 CIII ✉ 41 Rabat Road, Marsalforn ☎ 21553630

Mid-Range Hotels

PRICES

Expect to pay €100–€150 per night for a double room in a mid-range hotel.

Malta

BAYVIEW HOTEL

www.bayviewhotel.com
On the main waterfront strip at Sliema, this is a small tourist hotel with a useful location and not one but two pools (outdoor and indoor). Rooms are tidy, spacious and modern. There are three restaurants on site, plus an internet café.
✚ H5 ✉ 143 The Strand, Gzira-Sliema ☎ 21320216

THE DOLMEN HOTEL

www.dolmen.com.mt
This large resort hotel on the St. Paul's Bay waterfront has a good range of facilities, including restaurants, bars, a casino, spa, five pools, and a summer kid's club. There's also a small sandy beach just across the corniche.
✚ E3 ✉ Coast Road, Qawra, St. Paul's Bay ☎ 23552355

HOTEL KENNEDY NOVA

www.kennedynova.com
On the waterfront strip at the eastern end, as Sliema meets Gzira. You can choose from rooms or one-bedroom apartments. There's a good range of facilities, including restaurant, bar, pool, and fitness room with sauna. There are WiFi areas in reception and on the pool deck.
✚ G5 ✉ 116 The Strand, Gzira ☎ 21345480

HOTEL VALENTINA

www.hotelvalentina.com
In this small, contemporary hotel, on a residential street in the heart of the Paceville entertainment district, rooms have a minimalist feel, while the reception area oozes style with its steel staircase and pastel panel lighting. There's a breakfast room on site and the hotel owns The Avenue Restaurant close by, where residents get a discount. WiFi is free.
✚ G4 ✉ Shrieber Street, Paceville ☎ 21382232

MARITIM ANTONINE HOTEL & SPA

www.maritim.com.mt
This is a very comfortable, contemporary Italianate-style hotel with an excellent spa facility,

ECO-CERTIFICATION

Malta Tourism Authority has introduced an eco-certificate for hotels meeting criteria relating to energy conservation, waste management, water quality and noise levels. By early 2010, 18 establishments had been awarded the certificate. For current details of certified accommodation, go to www.mta.com.mt/eco-certification

the Aphrodite, on site. There's a good-sized pool and a verdant garden for relaxing. In the heart of Mellieħa town, the hotel is within walking distance of a range of restaurants.
✚ C3 ✉ Borg Olivier Street, Mellieħa ☎ 21520923

NEW TOWER PALACE HOTEL

www.newtowerpalacehotel.com
Equidistant between Valletta and the Paceville district, a rather dated exterior hides a bright three-star property that's preferred by many tour groups. There's an infinity-edge pool on the roof, and a restaurant and internet café on site.
✚ H5 ✉ Tower Road, Sliema ☎ 21337271

THE OSBORNE HOTEL

www.osbornehotel.com
The most stylish hotel within Valletta city walls, the Osborne boasts a small roof pool. The hotel has many testimonials dating from throughout the 20th century but refurbished all rooms in 2010. There's a restaurant and bar on site.
✚ c2 ✉ 50 South Street, Valletta ☎ 21243656

PARK HOTEL

www.parkhotel.com.mt
The rather dull entrance-way to the Park hides a comfortable, modern, four-star property with bright and airy communal spaces. Rooms could

benefit from some contemporary style touches but offer comfortable accommodation. There's an indoor spa-type pool, fitness centre, 24-hour café and a restaurant on site.

➕ H5 ✉ Graham Street, Sliema ☎ 21343780

THE RIVIERA RESORT & SPA
www.riviera.com.mt
Occupying a sheltered bay facing Comino Island, The Riviera is a small but well-equipped resort hotel with a range of sports facilities, including a summer dive school, and the expansive Elysium Spa offering hydro- and thalasso-therapy. It's 100m (110 yards) to the nearest sandy beach.

➕ B2 ✉ Marfa Bay, Mellieħa ☎ 21525900

ST. JULIAN'S BAY HOTEL
www.stjuliansbayhotel.com
The unassuming vestibule hides a stylish contemporary property that's just a little too big to be called 'boutique'. The interior has modern art around the spacious lobby, giving it a grander feel than its three official stars.

➕ G5 ✉ 48 Main Street, St. Julian's ☎ 21361163

SOLANA HOTEL & SPA
www.solanahotel.com
This mid-sized contemporary hotel, built in traditional Maltese style,

has comfortable and well-fitted rooms with modern decoration. The main pool is on the roof, along with a generous sun deck. An indoor pool with adjoining Jacuzzi, and a fitness room, make this a very good option for winter breaks.

➕ C3 ✉ Borg Olivier Street, Mellieħa ☎ 21522209

VICTORIA HOTEL
www.victoriahotel.com
Styled like a Victorian gentleman's club, there's even a pub on the ground floor in keeping with tradition. It's set in a residential area, a 10-minute walk from the Sliema waterfront. The Victoria shares spa and restaurant facilities with the five-star sister hotel next door, The Palace, so guests have an excellent choice of eateries on site.

➕ H5 ✉ Gorg Borg Olivier Street, Sliema ☎ 21334711

THE WATERFRONT HOTEL
www.waterfronthotelmalta.com
With a vast frontage overlooking the coast, this four-star hotel is a cut above others along the strand and attracts business clients eschewing the five-star options. Rooms are comfortable and well-furnished, and there's a pool and deck on the roof, and a choice of bars and restaurants.

➕ H5 ✉ The Strand, Gzira ☎ 21333434

Gozo
GRAND HOTEL
www.grandhotelmalta.com
Majestic views over the harbour at Mġarr and Gozo Channel from most of the rooms make this one of the best hotels in which to open your curtains in the morning. It's modern Italianate in style and is well furbished throughout. There's an excellent restaurant on site and a lovely pool.

➕ DIV ✉ Mġarr ☎ 21563840

ST. PATRICK'S HOTEL
www.vjborg.com
Set on the waterfront in the heart of picturesque Xlendi Bay, this small and welcoming hotel makes a comfortable base. Styled like an old Gozitan palace, some rooms face on to a traditional interior courtyard. There's a fine restaurant on site.

➕ BIV ✉ Marina Street, Xlendi ☎ 21562951

Luxury Hotels

PRICES

Expect to pay over €150 per night for a double room in a luxury hotel.

Malta

BOUTIQUE HOTEL JULIANI

www.hoteljuliani.com
The original boutique hotel on Malta and still the best, the Juliani is well placed for the entertainment district but is away from the resultant hubbub. There's a cool, contemporary feel.
G5 ⊠ 12 St. George's Road, St. Julian's
☎ 21388000

CORINTHIA PALACE HOTEL & SPA

www.corinthiahotels.com
Flagship of the Maltese CHI Group and voted the best hotel on Malta (World Travel Awards 2009), this luxurious property sits in the heart of the island in beautifully sculpted grounds. A true modern 'palace' oozing quality and comfort, the hotel has many facilities.
F6 ⊠ De Paule Avenue, Attard ☎ 21440301

GRAND HOTEL EXCELSIOR

www.excelsior.com.mt
This large five-star hotel offers 21st-century comforts and style, just steps from Valletta's bastions. There is a good range of restaurants and leisure facilities on site, and the spa is one of the best on the island.
b2 ⊠ Great Siege Road, Floriana ☎ 21250520

LE MÉRIDIEN ST. JULIAN'S HOTEL AND SPA

www.lemeridienmalta.com
Tumbling down the hillside, this contemporary resort hotel makes a dramatic first impression and the interior doesn't disappoint. The restaurants include the signature Villa Brasserie, set in a 19th-century pavilion.
G5 ⊠ 29 Main Street, Balluta Bay, St. Julian's
☎ 23110000

RADISSON BLU RESORT AND SPA, MALTA GOLDEN BAY

www.radissonblu.com
This large ultra-modern hotel stands sentinel over the sandy beach. There are dining options and bars, which is useful since there are no facilities within walking distance of the hotel in the evenings.
B4 ⊠ Golden Bay, Mellieħa ☎ 23561000

THE XARA PALACE

Built as a summerhouse in the 17th century, the Xara Palace opened in 1999, managed with understated charm by the Zammit Tabona family. It's the only Maltese hotel as yet to be included in the Relais & Chateaux umbrella of 475 luxury properties.

THE WESTIN DRAGONARA RESORT

www.starwoodhotels.com
This expansive resort occupies the tip of the Dragonara peninsula. Facilities include a well-stocked shopping promenade, and Malta's original casino.
G4 ⊠ Dragonara Road, St. Julian's ☎ 21381000

THE XARA PALACE

www.xarapalace.com.mt
This fabulous palace in the heart of the Citadel, dating from the 17th century, is a luxury boutique hotel (▷ panel). There's no pool, but some of the suites have a private terrace Jacuzzi.
D6 ⊠ Misrah il-Kunsill, Mdina ☎ 21450560

Gozo

KEMPINSKI SAN LAWRENZ

www.kempinski.com
Set around three pools, the traditional Gozitan hotel has three restaurants, two bars, and a spa that opened in 2010.
AIII ⊠ Triq ir-Roken, San Lawrenz ☎ 22110000

TA'CENC

www.vjborg.com
This five-star village-style hotel offers rooms in traditional *trulli* (stone 'bungalows'), set in verdant grounds. There is a good range of sports facilities here, and a private beach in a cove.
CIV ⊠ Sannat
☎ 21556819 ⊕ Easter–Oct

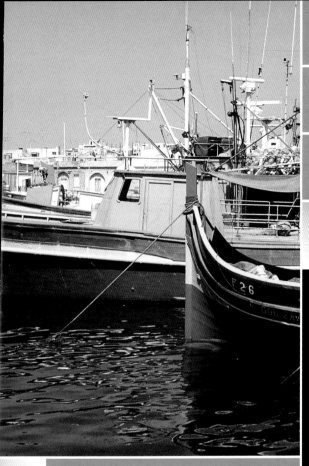

This section is packed with practical information on planning a trip to Malta and Gozo, finding your way around once you get there, tips on pronunciation, and the historical highlights.

Planning Ahead

When to Go

Malta's Mediterranean climate means summers are hot, but this is the busiest time of year. To avoid the crowds, visit between October and April; great for walking and sightseeing, though boat trips don't always run. Gozo is very quiet in the winter; many facilities and hotels are closed.

AVERAGE DAILY MAXIMUM TEMPERATURES

JAN	FEB	MAR	APR	MAY	JUN	JUL	AUG	SEP	OCT	NOV	DEC
15°C	15°C	16°C	19°C	23°C	28°C	30°C	31°C	28°C	24°C	20°C	17°C
59°F	59°F	61°F	66°F	73°F	82°F	86°F	88°F	82°F	75°F	68°F	63°F

Spring (March to May) is dry, with temperatures rising rapidly as summer approaches.
Summer (June to August) is hot, dry and sunny, with temperatures often above 30°C (86°F). Humidity is high, which can make nights uncomfortable without air-conditioning.
Autumn (September to October) brings shorter days, so the temperature drops and October sees more rainfall then any other month.
Winter (November to February) is mild; temperatures rarely fall below 10°C (50°F) and average 15°C (59°F), though the wind chill can make it feel colder. Days are character- ized as sunshine mixed with rain showers.

WHAT'S ON

February *Feast of St. Paul's Shipwreck* (10 Feb): The figure of Saint Paul is carried through Valletta.
March/April *Holy Week*: On Good Friday, solemn processions are held in 17 towns around Malta and Gozo. Some Catholics dress as biblical characters or as penitents. Easter Sunday has happier processions, as the statue of Christ Resurrected is carried around streets close to the church, often taking a run at speed to get back through the church doors.
June *Sette Giugno* (7 Jun): Wreath-laying at a

statue outside the Auberge de Castille in Valletta, commemorating victims of an anti-British uprising in 1919.
Feast of St. Peter and St. Paul (29 Jun): A spectacular procession on the feast day of the two saints in Nadur, Gozo.
August *Feast of the Assumption* (15 Aug): Major *festas* at Attard, Għaxaq, Gudja, Mġarr, Mosta, Mqabba, Qrendi and Victoria.
September *Victory Day* (8 Sep): Commemorating the end of the Great Siege in 1565, and the second Siege of Malta in 1943, both of

which broke on the same day. There are boat races in Grand Harbour.
Independence Day (21 Sep): A military parade and the laying of wreaths by politicians in Valletta and Victoria. There's also a mass by the Bishop of Malta.

Malta and Gozo Online

www.visitmalta.com
The official Malta Tourist Authority website is easy to use and is full of useful, practical, historical and cultural information on all three Maltese islands. It's also updated regularly.

www.islandofgozo.org
The official Gozo website has 'what to do and see' information and a 'where to stay' section. A simple interactive map of the island helps you get started.

www.wirtartna.org
Malta Heritage Trust operates several attractions around the islands and is in the process of renovating others. The website gives background information on the foundation and practical information on visiting the sites.

www.heritagemalta.org
Heritage Malta manages many of the prime ancient and historical sites and the major museums. It has practical information and some background history about each of its properties.

www.timesofmalta.com
The website of Malta's leading English language newspaper keeps you up to date with all that's happening on the island and is a place to start research about current politics and daily life.

www.malta.com
This is a commercial magazine-style site with information about what to do and see, and where to stay, together with some property and business contacts.

www.gov.mt
The official Government of Malta website features information in English about visas, embassies, and rules and regulations for property purchases and retirement or relocation to Malta.

GETTING ONLINE

Most mid-range to luxury hotels offer WiFi or broadband access in the room or reception area. There are an increasing number of WiFi hotspots, including some cafés and restaurants, and local authorities such as Valletta and Sliema are also creating free hotspots in parks and squares.

INTERNET CAFÉS

There are few internet cafés where you can pay for internet access. Details of two cafés on Malta are given below.

Hackers Café
www.hackersmalta.com
✉ 2 J Borg Street, Msida
☎ 21231285
🕐 Apr–Sep Mon–Fri 10–6, Sat 10–3; Oct–Mar Mon–Tue, Thu–Fri 9–7, Wed 9–6, Sat 9–3
💶 €3 per hour

Point de Vue
✉ 5 Saqqajja, Rabat
☎ 21454117
🕐 Daily 9–9
💶 €3.50 per hour

Getting There

ENTRY REQUIREMENTS

EU citizens do not require a visa to enter Malta. Visitors from Australia, Canada, New Zealand and the USA do not require a visa for stays of up to 90 days. All other nationalities should consult the Malta government website (www.gov.mt) or their Maltese Embassy. Always check the latest requirements before you travel, as they are subject to change.

INSURANCE

EU nationals are entitled to emergency medical treatment. Make sure you carry a European Health Insurance Card (EHIC) to prove your entitlement. In the UK, further information and application forms are available from www.ehic.org. uk or ☎ 0845 606 2030, and in the Republic of Ireland see www.hse.ie. A comprehensive travel insurance policy is advised for all travellers. Since the EHIC only allows entitlement to emergency services and does not cover items like emergency repatriation, a comprehensive travel insurance policy is still advised for EU citizens. A travel insurance policy will also cover issues like flight delays, and will provide cover for damaged, lost or stolen personal items.

AIRPORT

Malta has one airport (IATA Code MLA) for international access, at Luqa (pronounced Lu-a). Originally a British Royal Air Force base, it opened as a commercial airport in 1992. Airport operations and the terminal are modern and efficient. There is no airport on Gozo.

ARRIVING BY AIR

Malta International Airport (www.maltairport. com) is 5km (3 miles) south of Valletta. Air Malta (☎ 21662211; www.airmalta.com) is the country's national carrier and operates services to a network of European cities (including Dublin), and to Belfast City, Birmingham, Glasgow, London Gatwick and Heathrow, and Manchester in the UK. Other airlines with services from the UK/Republic of Ireland to Malta include low-cost easyJet (www.easyjet.com) from London Gatwick, Manchester, Liverpool and Newcastle; BMI (www.flybmi.com) with services from London Gatwick and Heathrow; and Ryanair (www.ryanair.com) with services from Bournemouth, Bristol, Edinburgh, Leeds, Luton and Dublin.

From the airport, it's no more than an hour's drive to all parts of the island. The inexpensive (€1.16) public bus service (route 8) travels from the airport through Gudja, Għaxaq, Tarxien, Marsa and Floriana, before terminating at the bus station in Valletta. There are three services per hour from Monday to Friday 6am to 9pm, with fewer at the weekend. However, the bus doesn't travel through any of the areas with tourist facilities and though it would be possible to take another service to your resort from Valletta, this airport bus is most useful for visitors staying in hotels in Valletta itself.

TAXIS
Taxis are available to meet all flights and operate on fixed rates. You can prepay for journeys in the Welcomer's Hall (arrivals hall). Sample fares are €15.75 to Valletta, €20.75 to Sliema, St. Julian's and Paceville, and €25.75 to Buġibba and St. Paul's Bay—all fares carry an additional administrative fee of €0.75.

CAR RENTAL
There are car rental desks in the arrivals hall, including international brands such as Europcar (www.europcar.com.mt), Hertz (www.hertz. com.mt) and Budget (www.budget.com.mt).

PACKAGE TOURS
If you travel by package tour you are likely to be transported to your accommodation by coach, so check with your travel company.

INTER-ISLAND TRAVEL
You can travel from Malta to Gozo either by air or by sea. Harbour Air (☎ 21228302; www.harbourairmalta.com) offers a scheduled seaplane service from Grand Harbour at Valletta to Mġarr harbour on Gozo. Depending on the time of year, there are three to six services per day and the flight takes around 20 minutes. Fares are €80 for a return trip. Passenger ferries run from Ċirkewwa on the northwest coast of Malta to Mġarr on southeast Gozo. The Gozo Channel Company (☎ 21561622; www.gozochannel.com) operates all services, which cater for vehicle and foot traffic. Services run 24 hours per day year round, with services every 45 minutes during the day, and the journey takes 25 minutes. Fares are €15.70 for a car and driver, plus €4.65 per passenger/ foot passenger.

FERRIES FROM ITALY

Valletta is linked to Italy by several passenger/vehicle ferry services. Grandi Navi Veloci (www.gnv.it) links Valletta with Genoa (and Tunis) in a weekly service. Grimaldi Lines (www. grimaldi-ferries.com) has services to Civitavecchia and Catania. Virtu Ferries (www. virtuferries.com) runs services to and from two ports in Sicily—Pozzallo by fast catamaran, and Catania.

CRUISING TO MALTA

Malta is one of the Mediterranean's busiest and most popular cruise ports. If you want to 'Cruise and Stay' (start/end a cruise here with some time in a hotel before or after your shipboard itinerary), Costa Cruises (www.costacruise.com) base many of their summer sailings out of Valletta. Companies which use Malta as a port of call are Louis Cruises (www.louiscruises. com), Fred Olsen Cruises (www.fredolsencruises.com), Silver Sea Cruises (www. silversea.com), Norwegian Cruise Lines (www.ncl.com) and Holland America (www. hollandamerica.com). Length of stay in port ranges from four to ten hours—so it's a whistle-stop tour.

Getting Around

VISITORS WITH DISABILITIES

Only 10 per cent of buses currently have disabled access and these don't run on set routes at set times, but during 2011 new stock will be introduced on all routes. New-build properties meet EU policy guidelines on access. Some historic buildings have ramps and elevators. However, access remains difficult in some areas, not least in trying to get up and down the high roadside kerbs across the islands, and the steps that characterize Valletta's streets.

SIGHTSEEING BUS SERVICES

Malta Sightseeing Buses operate two hop on–hop off open-top services with commentary: one covering the southeast of the island (the red route), the other the north and west (the blue route). Both depart from Sliema ferry dock and stop at all the major tourist attractions on their route. Tickets are €15 and are valid for the whole day. The buses depart on the hour (Mon–Sat 9–3, Sun 10–1). On Gozo, a route departs from Mġarr ferry dock daily on the half-hour (9.30–2.30). Tickets are €15. For more details ☎ 21694967 or see www.maltasightseeing.com

BUSES

Both Malta and Gozo have a network of daytime bus services that are inexpensive and efficient. In 2011, the network is due to be transferred to commercial ownership and timetables may be subject to change at this time. Check on the website (www.atp.com.mt for Malta or www.gozo.gov.mt for Gozo) or with local tourist offices for the latest information.

On Malta Valletta acts as a hub. From the central bus station there are services to every settlement, though these may run only once or twice per day. Major towns such as Rabat and Mosta, and along the coast through Sliema, have several services per day. The majority of services run from 5am to 7pm, though some services, such as to Sliema/St. Julian's, run until 10pm. Night services link Valletta, the Three Cities area, Mellieħa, Ċirkewwa (for the Gozo ferry) and Mosta with the tourist strip of Sliema, St. Julian's and Paceville on Friday and Saturday nights, until 3am. In summer this service runs nightly. Fares are inexpensive, ranging from €0.35 for one fare stage to €0.58 for three fare stages. Direct Express routes cost €1.16. There are also multiple-fare tickets priced at €3.49 for one day, €9.32 for three days, €11.65 for five days and €13.98 for seven days. These cards allow travel from 5.30am to 11pm on any given day or consecutive days. Tickets can be bought from the driver, from ticket kiosks or from ticket dispensing machines. For further information see the website (www.atp.com.mt).

On Gozo A small number of bus services link the major towns and resorts on Gozo, with a hub at the bus terminus in Victoria. Services run from around 5am until 5pm but some services to the coastal resorts run until 11pm during the summer. There are fewer services in the winter. For further information see www.gozo.gov.mt or ☎ 21559344 for general enquiries and ☎ 21562040 for schedule enquiries. Bus service 25 runs from Victoria terminus to the Mġarr

ferry (Jun–Sep Mon–Sat 5.30am–7.45pm,
Sun 7.15–7.15; Oct–May daily 5.30am–7pm).
Further services operate between Mġarr and
Victoria (Jun–Sep Mon–Sat 7.15am–8pm, Sun
7.15–7.15; Oct–May daily 7.15am–7.30pm).
Fares are €0.47 per journey, but those travelling
between 5am and 8am pay only €0.30. Tickets
can be purchased on the bus.

DRIVING

Driving is the best way to see Malta and Gozo.
Car rental prices are reasonable but cars are
not always new. Check for previous damage
before signing for the vehicle. Don't forget:
you'll need your driving licence. UK drivers will
need both the photo licence and the paper
licence. Carry the rental agreement, licence and
your ID with you when you are in the car.

Driving Tips
● Traffic drives on the left.
● Speed limits are 80kph (50mph) on the open
road and 50kph (30mph) in built-up areas.
● Speed cameras are common and fines will
be added to your car rental bill if you don't pay
them before you leave. You can pay online.
● Major roads are in good condition but minor
roads may be potholed and some country roads
are hard-packed ground, not asphalt.
● Kerbs are high and this can cause you to catch
wheels or side panels when parking.
● Roads are prone to flooding in rainstorms.
● Parking is a major problem.
● There is little parking on the outskirts of
Valletta. Other towns have strict parking regulations. Abide by these or you will be ticketed.

TAXIS

Licensed taxis are white and can pick up fares
anywhere except at bus stops. Short journeys
should cost €5 or €6; the journey from the
airport to anywhere on Malta is no more than
€29.75. Contact Malta Taxi Online (www.mal-
tataxionline.com or ☎ 99977761) or Malta Taxi
Cab (www.maltataxicab.com or ☎ 21489991).

many little lanes. Once you
make the effort to climb
to the central plateau, it's
easy to explore by bicycle.
All the main resorts have
rental shops. Try On 2
Wheels (☎ 21561503;
www.on2wheelsgozo.com)
in Marsalforn, which has
bicycles for rent for around
€10 per day, and you can
rent helmets, child seats and
lights as extras.

TOURS

Organized tours can be a
great way to see both Malta
and Gozo, especially if you
don't want to drive. You'll
travel in a minibus or full-
sized coach, depending on
group size. In addition, there
are lots of day cruises taking
in the Blue Lagoon (▷ 97).
There's a good choice of
providers and keen price
competition, or contact
Zarb Tours (☎ 21489991;
www.zarbcoaches.com).

MAPS

Tourist offices in Malta and
Gozo have simple maps of
the islands and of Valletta
and Victoria. But for touring, Kompass produces a
1:25,000 scale detailed map.
For more details visit
www.kompass.at

...tial Facts

● Police, Fire and Ambulance
☎ 112

MONEY

● Malta uses the euro (€) as its currency. Each euro is made up of 100 cents. Notes come in denominations of 5, 10, 20, 50, 100, 200 and 500 euros; coins come in denominations of 1, 2, 5, 10, 20, 50 cents, and 1 and 2 euros.

5 euros

10 euros

50 euros

100 euros

TOURIST OFFICES

✉ Merchants Street, Valletta, Malta
☎ 22915440

✉ Trigrija Palazz, Republic Street, Victoria, Gozo
☎ 21561419

ELECTRICITY

Malta uses 240 volts, 50 cycles. Plugs are British three-pin style. European appliances will need an adaptor. American appliances will need a converter (not practical).

HEALTH AND SAFETY

Medical care in Malta is of a good standard. Staff speak excellent English. On Malta, Mater Dei Hospital is at Tal-Qroqq, Msida (☎ 25450000). Gozo General Hospital is in Victoria (☎ 21561600). Pharmacists speak good English, and they can advise on treatments for minor conditions. Pharmacies are well stocked with medicines. Malta is a safe destination by international standards. Women will not be hassled if they enter a bar or restaurant alone. It's safe to walk in streets after dark, though it's sensible not to wander around alone at night. Many hotels have single rooms and special rates for singles booking a double room. Malta is not a heavy crime area but precautions are always sensible: Don't carry large amounts of cash or valuables; don't leave anything on show in rental cars; don't leave anything valuable unattended in public places, such as cafés or on the beach. Occasional problems of drunkenness and rowdiness can develop in Paceville, especially at weekends.

NATIONAL HOLIDAYS

1 Jan: New Year's Day; 10 Feb: Feast of St. Paul's Shipwreck; 19 Mar: Feast of St. Joseph; 31 Mar: Freedom Day; Mar/Apr: Good Friday; 1 May: Labour Day; 7 Jun: Sette Guigno; 29 Jun: Feast of St. Peter and St. Paul; 15 Aug: Feast of the Assumption; 8 Sep: Feast of Our Lady of Victories; 21 Sep: Independence Day; 8 Dec: Feast of the Immaculate Conception; 13 Dec: Republic Day; 25 Dec: Christmas Day.

NEWSPAPERS AND MAGAZINES

The main English-language Maltese newspapers are the *Times of Malta*, and the *Malta Independent*, both published daily. The main

English-language tabloids, international press and major magazines can be purchased at newsagents at a price premium over standard UK and US prices.

OPENING HOURS
● Shops: Mon–Sat 9–1, 4–7. Some tourist shops open through the day and on Sundays.
● Museums: Daily 9–5.
● Post offices: Malta Valletta office Mon–Fri 8.15–3.45, Sat 8.15–12.30; Malta branch offices Mon–Fri 8–1, 1.30–3.30. Gozo Victoria office Mon–Fri 8.15–4.30, Sat 8.15–12.30; Gozo branch offices Mon–Sat 7.30–12.45.
● Banks: Mon–Fri 8.30–1.30 or 2. Some open extended hours and on Saturday mornings.

PLACES OF WORSHIP
Every village or town has a Catholic church. For Anglican services on Malta visit St. Paul's Pro Cathedral in Valletta or Holy Trinity Church in Sliema. Contact the Anglican community for information about services on Gozo. For more details visit www.anglicanmalta.org. There is one mosque: Corradino Mosque in Paola.

POST OFFICES
Malta Post operates reliable postal services in Malta and Gozo. The main office on Malta is at Castille Place, Valletta; on Gozo, the main office is at 129 Republic Street, Victoria. Stamps for postcards (currently €0.37 to Europe, €0.51 to North America and South Africa, and €0.86 to Australia and New Zealand) can be bought at stationers and souvenir shops.

TELEPHONES
The international code for Malta and Gozo is 00356. Local numbers are eight digits long. Public phones operate with a card system. Mobile coverage is good; the major provider is Vodafone. To phone home from Malta use the following codes (omit the first 0 from the local number): UK 0044; Ireland 00353; Germany 0049; USA and Canada 001.

SMOKING
● Smoking is not allowed in enclosed public spaces.

EMBASSIES AND CONSULATES
● UK High Commission
✉ Whitehall Mansions, Ta'Xbiex Seafront
☎ 23230000
● Ireland
✉ Whitehall Mansions, Ta'Xbiex Seafront
☎ 21334774
● USA
✉ Development House, 3rd Floor, St. Anne House, Floriana ☎ 25614000

TIPPING
● Service charge is not automatically added to restaurant and bar bills but in more expensive establishments it may be included. If service charge is not included, leave around 10 per cent. In bars, leave loose change.

ETIQUETTE
● Malta is a conservative country. Only wear beachwear on the beach or by the pool.
● When visiting churches, don't wear shorts or short skirts, cover shoulders, take off hats. Switch off mobile phones.

Language

Maltese and English are the official languages of Malta and Gozo. Almost everyone speaks English but it is Maltese that is normally heard on the streets and that predominates in the media. Maltese comprises a vast element of words of Italian, French and English origin. The alphabet consists of 29 characters: a, b, ċ (as ch in 'church'), c, d, e, f, ġ (as g in 'George'), g, ħ (as h in 'house'), h, i, j, k, l, m, n, għ (a single letter and usually silent), o, p, q, r, s, t, u, v, w, x, ż (as z in 'zebra') and z. Menus are all in English but road signs are, for the most part, Maltese. Here are some words and phrases that may be helpful.

USEFUL WORDS AND PHRASES	
yes	iva
no	le
please	jekk jogħġbok
thank you	grazzi
hello	merħba
goodbye	saħħa
goodnight	il-lejl it-tajjeb
sorry	jiddispjaċini
help!	ajjut!
today	illum
tomorrow	għada
yesterday	il-bieraħ
how much?	kemm?
expensive	għoli
open	miftuħ
closed	magħluqh

EATING OUT	
restaurant	restorant
café	café
table	mejda
menu	menu
set menu	menu fiss
wine list	lista ta' l-inbid
lunch	kolazjonn
dinner	ikla
starter	starter
main course	ikla
dessert	deserta
drink	xorb
water	ilma
coffee	kafħ
waiter	waiter
the bill	kontl

ACCOMMODATION

hotel	lukanda
room	kamra
...single/double	singlu/doppja
...one/two nights	lejl/żewġ iljieli
...per person/	kull persuna/
...per room	kull kamra
reservation	riserva
rate	rata
breakfast	l-ewwel ikla tal-jum
toilet/bathroom	kamra tal banju
shower	doċċa
balcony	gallarija
reception	reception
key	ċavetta
room service	servizz fil-kamra
chambermaid	kamrieraa

TRANSPORT

aeroplane	ajruplan
airport	ajruport
bus	karozza tal-linja
bus station	stazzjon tal karozza tal-linja
railway station	stazzjon tal ferrovija
ferry terminal	vapur terminal
ticket	biljett
...return/single	single/bur-ritorn
...first/second class	l-ewwl/tiieni klassi
ticket office	uffiċju tal biljetti
timetable	orarju
seat	seat/post
non-smoking	tpejjipx
reserved	riservat

MONEY

bank	bank
post office	posta
cashier	kaxxier
foreign exchange	uffiċju tal-kambju
foreign currency	flus barranin
exchange rate	rata tal-kambju
commission charge	senserija
pound sterling	lira sterlina
American dollar	dollaru Amerikan
banknote	karta tal-flus
coin	munita
credit card	karta ta' kredtu
cheque book	cheque book

Timeline

5200BC–4000BC The Għar Dalam era sees the first traces of human settlement.

c.4000BC–2500BC The Temple Building civilization develops and thrives throughout the time archaeologists know as the Copper Age. This civilization disappears abruptly at c.2500BC.

2500BC–c.800BC The Bronze Age leaves cart ruts and dolmen across the islands.

c.600BC Phoenicians settle on the island and carve tomb complexes.

257BC Roman forces raze Phoenician settlements on Malta during the Punic Wars.

218BC Malta part of the Roman Empire.

AD60 St. Paul is shipwrecked on Malta and converts the Roman governor to Christianity, founding a Christian community.

500–800 The Byzantine Empire, based in Constantinople, controls Malta.

870–1090 Arab rule.

1090–1530 The fiefdom of Malta passes to western European feudal noble dynasties.

1530 Charles V of Spain grants Malta to the Knights Hospitallers of the Order of St. John in perpetuity. They settle in Birgu (now Vittoriosa).

KNIGHTS HOSPITALLERS

Officially named The Sovereign Military Hospitaller Order of St. John of Jerusalem of Rhodes and of Malta, the Order was founded c.1048, when Christians built a convent and hospital in Muslim Jerusalem. The Order tended the sick, and during the Crusades they defended the sick, as their military role.

Mosaics in the Roman baths, Rabat (left and middle); Seige Bell Memorial, commemorating those who lost their lives defending the convoys in World War II (right)

1565 Ottoman forces attempt to take the island and the Great Siege ensues. After two months, the Knights repulse Ottoman forces.

1566 The city of Valletta is founded.

1614 Second Ottoman invasion is repelled.

1798 Napoleon invades Malta. The Knights are ejected. The French loot treasures.

1800 French surrender; British occupation.

1814 The Treaty of Paris declares Malta a British Crown Colony.

1835 The first Maltese constitution gives the people some representation.

1942–43 During World War II, the second Siege of Malta sees 6,000 tonnes of bombs dropped on the island by Axis forces.

1964 Malta achieves independence within the British Commonwealth.

1974 Malta becomes a Republic.

1990 Pope John Paul II's official visit.

2004 Malta becomes a member of the EU.

2008 The Euro becomes official currency.

2010 Pope Benedict XVI's official visit.

PAY THE RENT

When Charles V of Spain granted the Maltese islands to the Knights Hospitallers, he asked for a token rent: one falcon to be delivered yearly. The Maltese Falcon was later used by Dashiell Hammett as the title of his best-selling detective story, turned into a famous film-noir starring Humphrey Bogart in 1941.

NURSE OF THE MEDITERRANEAN

During the 19th and early 20th centuries, British soldiers and seamen injured in combat during numerous skirmishes and colonial battles, including many in the Crimean War and World War I, came to Malta to be treated and to recuperate. This earned the island the nickname 'Nurse of the Mediterranean'.

Ghar Dalam holds the earliest evidence of life on Malta (left); an exhibit in the National War Museum (middle); the George Cross awarded to islanders (right)

Index

TWINPACK
Malta & Gozo

WRITTEN BY Lindsay Bennett
COVER DESIGN Catherine Murray
DESIGN WORK Lesley Mitchell
INDEXER Marie Lorimer
IMAGE RETOUCHING AND REPRO Sarah Montgomery
PROJECT EDITOR Lodestone Publishing Limited
SERIES EDITOR Marie-Claire Jefferies

© **AA MEDIA LIMITED 2011**

Colour separation by AA Digital Department
Printed and bound by Leo Paper Products, China

A CIP catalogue record for this book is available from the British Library.

ISBN 978-0-7495-6807-8

Published by AA Publishing, a trading name of AA Media Limited, whose registered office is Fanum House, Basing View, Basingstoke, Hampshire RG21 4EA. Registered number 06112600.

Front cover image: © Phil Pryce/Alamy
Back cover images: (i) AA/A Kouprianoff; (ii) AA/C Sawyer; (iii) AA/W Voysey; (iv) AA/P Enticknap

A04027
Maps in this title produced from mapping © MAIRDUMONT / Falk Verlag 2011

The Automobile Association would like to thank the following photographers, companies and picture libraries for their assistance in the preparation of this book.

Abbreviations for the pictures credits are as follows – (t) top; (b) bottom; (c) centre; (l) left; (r) right; (AA) AA World Travel Library.

1 AA/P Enticknap; 2 AA/A Kouprianoff; 3 AA/A Kouprianoff; 4t AA/A Kouprianoff; 4c AA/P Enticknap; 5t AA/A Kouprianoff; 5c AA/A Kouprianoff; 6t AA/A Kouprianoff; 6cl AA/W Voysey; 6c AA/A Kouprianoff; 6cr AA/P Enticknap; 6bl AA/P Enticknap; 6bc AA/P Enticknap; 6br AA/P Enticknap; 7t AA/A Kouprianoff; 7lcl AA/P Enticknap; 7cl AA/P Enticknap; 7cr AA/P Enticknap; 7rcr AA/P Enticknap; 7bl AA/P Enticknap; 7bc AA/A Kouprianoff; 7br AA/W Voysey; 8 AA/A Kouprianoff; 9 AA/A Kouprianoff; 10t AA/A Kouprianoff; 10/11t AA/T Carter; 10ct AA/P Enticknap; 10cb AA/P Enticknap; 10/11b AA/J A Tims; 11t AA/A Kouprianoff; 11c AA/P Bennett; 12t AA/A Kouprianoff; 12tct AA; 12ct AA/A Kouprianoff; 12cb AA/A Kouprianoff; 12b AA; 13t AA/A Kouprianoff; 13tct Digital Vision; 13ct AA/J Love; 13cb AA/P Enticknap; 13b AA/P Enticknap; 14t AA/A Kouprianoff; 14tct AA/P Enticknap; 14ct AA/P Enticknap; 14cb AA/A Kouprianoff; 14b AA/P Enticknap; 15t AA/A Kouprianoff; 15b AA/P Enticknap; 16t AA/A Kouprianoff; 16ct AA/P Enticknap; 16cb AA/A Kouprianoff; 16b AA/W Voysey; 17t AA/A Kouprianoff; 17tct AA/A Kouprianoff; 17ct AA/P Enticknap; 17cb AA/P Enticknap; 18t AA/A Kouprianoff; 18ct © Imagebroker/Alamy; 18c AA/D Vincent; 18b AA/P Enticknap; 19t AA/P Enticknap; 19ct AA/P Enticknap; 19cb AA/A Kouprianoff; 19b © M J Perris/Alamy; 20/21 AA/A Kouprianoff; 24l © Andrew Holt/Alamy; 24r © Andrew Holt/Alamy; 25l AA/A Kouprianoff; 25r AA/A Kouprianoff; 26/27 AA/A Kouprianoff; 27 AA/P Enticknap; 28/29 AA/A Kouprianoff; 30/31 © CuboImages srl/Alamy; 31t © Imagebroke/Alamy; 31b © Robert Harding Picture Library Ltd/Alamy; 32l © John Stark/Alamy; 32r © Tony French/Alamy; 33l © Andrew Holt/Alamy; 33r © The Art Archive/Alamy; 34l ©Nikreates/Alamy; 34r AA/W Voysey; 35l AA/P Enticknap; 35r AA/A Kouprianoff; 36t AA/A Kouprianoff; 36bl AA/P Enticknap; 36br AA/W Voysey; 37t AA/A Kouprianoff; 37b © Imagebroker/Alamy; 38t AA/A Kouprianoff; 38b AA/P Enticknap; 39t AA/A Kouprianoff; 39b © Simon Reddy/Alamy; 40 AA/A Kouprianoff; 41 AA/P Enticknap; 42 AA/P Enticknap; 43 AA/A Kouprianoff; 44 AA/C Sawyer; 45 AA/P Enticknap; 48l AA/P Enticknap; 48r AA/P Enticknap; 49l AA/A Kouprianoff; 49r AA/P Enticknap; 50/51 © Robert Estall Photo Agency/Alamy; 51 © Robert Estall Photo Agency/Alamy; 52 AA/W Voysey; 52/53 AA/W Voysey; 54 AA/P Enticknap; 54/55t AA/P Enticknap; 54/55b AA/A Kouprianoff; 55t AA/P Enticknap; 55b AA/A Kouprianoff; 56l AA/W Voysey; 56/57t AA/W Voysey; 56br AA/A Kouprianoff; 57t AA/P Enticknap; 57bl AA/A Kouprianoff; 57br AA/A Kouprianoff; 58t AA/W Voysey; 58b AA/A Kouprianoff; 59t AA/W Voysey; 59b AA/P Enticknap; 60t AA/W Voysey; 60b AA/A Kouprianoff; 61t AA/W Voysey; 61bl AA/W Voysey; 61br AA/P Enticknap; 62t AA/W Voysey; 62b AA/A Kouprianoff; 63t AA/W Voysey; 63bl AA/W Voysey; 63br AA/P Enticknap; 64 AA/A Kouprianoff; 65 AA/A Kouprianoff; 66 AA/P Enticknap; 67 AA/A Kouprianoff; 68 AA/C Sawyer; 69 AA/A Kouprianoff; 72l AA/P Enticknap; 72tr AA/A Kouprianoff; 72/73 AA/A Kouprianoff; 73t AA/P Enticknap; 73c AA/A Kouprianoff; 74l AA/W Voysey; 74c AA/A Kouprianoff; 74r AA/A Kouprianoff; 75l AA/A Kouprianoff; 75r AA/A Kouprianoff; 76l © Victor Paul Borg/Alamy; 76r © Travel Division Images/Alamy; 77l AA/P Enticknap; 77r AA/A Kouprianoff; 78l © Ian Dagnall/Alamy; 78r AA/A Kouprianoff; 79 AA/P Enticknap; 80t AA/P Enticknap; 80bl AA/A Kouprianoff; 80br © Greg Balfour Evans/Alamy; 81t AA/P Enticknap; 81b © Victor Paul Borg/Alamy; 82t AA/P Enticknap; 82b AA/P Enticknap; 83t AA/P Enticknap; 83b AA/A Kouprianoff; 84t AA/P Enticknap; 84b AA/A Kouprianoff; 85t AA/P Enticknap; 85bl AA/A Kouprianoff; 85br AA/A Kouprianoff; 86 AA/P Enticknap; 87 AA/P Enticknap; 88 AA/P Enticknap; 89 AA/A Kouprianoff; 90 AA/C Sawyer; 91 © Imagebroker/Alamy; 94 AA/A Kouprianoff; 94/95 AA/P Enticknap; 96/97 © Slick Shoots/Alamy; 97 AA/W Voysey; 98 AA/P Enticknap; 99t AA/P Enticknap; 99c AA/P Enticknap; 100l © Greg Balfour Evans/Alamy; 100r AA/A Kouprianoff; 101t AA/D Vincent; 101b AA/A Kouprianoff; 102 AA/P Enticknap; 103 AA/P Enticknap; 104 AA/P Enticknap; 105 AA/A Kouprianoff; 106 AA/C Sawyer; 107 AA/A Kouprianoff; 108t AA/C Sawyer; 108ct AA/P Enticknap; 108c AA/P Enticknap; 108bc AA/P Enticknap; 109 AA/C Sawyer; 110 AA/C Sawyer; 111 AA/C Sawyer; 112 AA/C Sawyer 113 AA/A Kouprianoff; 114t AA/D Vincent; 114b AA/A Kouprianoff; 115 AA/D Vincent; 116 AA/D Vincent; 117 AA/D Vincent; 118 AA/D Vincent; 119 AA/D Vincent; 120t AA/D Vincent; 120l European Central Bank; 121 AA/D Vincent; 122t AA/D Vincent; 122b AA/P Enticknap; 123t AA/D Vincent; 123b Photodisc; 124t AA/D Vincent; 124bl AA/P Enticknap; 124bc AA/P Enticknap; 124br AA/D Vincent; 125t AA/D Vincent; 125bl AA/P Enticknap; 125bc AA/A Kouprianoff; 125br AA/W Voysey

Every effort has been made to trace the copyright holders, and we apologise in advance for any accidental errors. We would be happy to apply the corrections in the following edition of this publication.